RETRIEVING THE *American Past*

A CUSTOMIZED U.S. HISTORY READER
Dr. David Dzurec
University of Scranton
History 110

D1416963

Pearson Custom Publishing

New York   Boston   San Francisco
London   Toronto   Sydney   Tokyo   Singapore   Madrid
Mexico City   Munich   Paris   Cape Town   Hong Kong   Montreal

Senior Vice President, Editorial and Marketing: Patrick F. Boles
Senior Sponsoring Editor: Natalie Danner
Development Editors: Katherine R. Gehan and Mary Kate Paris
Editorial Assistant: Jill Johnson
Marketing Manager: Nathan Wilbur
Operations Manager: Eric M. Kenney
Database Product Manager: Jennifer Berry
Rights Manager: Katie Huha
Art Director and Cover Designer: Renée Sartell

Cover Art: Courtesy of Library of Congress and the Chicago History Museum.

**Pearson
Custom Publishing**
is a division of

www.pearsonhighered.com

ISBN 10: 0-536-55557-5
ISBN 13: 978-0-536-55557-1

CONTRIBUTORS

Senior Editor
Saul Cornell

Managing Editor
David Staley

Copy Editor
Ann Heiss

Assistant Managing Editor
Meredith Clark-Wiltz

Contributing Editors

Tyler Anbinder
Kenneth J. Andrien
Jean Harvey Baker
Michael Les Benedict
Mansel Blackford
Paul C. Bowers
Rowland Brucken
John D. Buenker
John C. Burnham
Joan E. Cashin
William R. Childs
Albert J. Churella
Steven Conn
Saul Cornell
Nick Cullather
Jeanette Davis
Merton L. Dillon
Daniel Feller
Charles Coleman Finlay
Emily Greenwald
Mark Grimsley
Bernard N. Grindel
Peter L. Hahn
James Hansen
Susan M. Hartmann
Mary Ann Heiss
Earl J. Hess
Michael J. Hogan
R. Douglas Hurt

Bruce Karhoff
Michael Kazin
Terence Kehoe
K. Austin Kerr
Frank Lambert
Valerie Mendoza
James McCaffrey
Allan R. Millett
Pamela J. Mills
Daniel Nelson
Margaret E. Newell
Josef Ostyn
Carla Gardina Pestana
Patrick D. Reagan
Randolph A. Roth
Hal K. Rothman
John A. M. Rothney
Leila J. Rupp
Richard D. Shiels
David Sicilia
C. Edward Skeen
Amy L. S. Staples
David L. Stebenne
David Steigerwald
Marshall F. Stevenson, Jr.
Warren R. Van Tine
Christopher Waldrep
J. Samuel Walker

Your *Retrieving the American Past* purchase includes access to online resources designed to complement your readings. This Companion Website is located at the following URL:

http://www.pearsoncustom.com/dbrtap/rtap/student

When prompted, enter the User Name: **rtapstudent** and Password: **rtaplearn**

(*Note:* The User Name and Password are case-sensitive, so be sure to use upper and lower case characters exactly as shown above.)

Once logged in, you will have access to the following resources:

- *Link Library.* A collection of vetted web links, organized by key terms and historical figures, which offer you background and context for many of the selections you'll be reading.

- *Documents.* Access (via links) to the full text of historical documents, which can furnish a backdrop to events that might have preceded, or followed, their drafting.

- *The Writing Process.* Advice that can aid you during the writing process. Included are guidelines and suggestions for each phase of writing, from start to finish.

- *Plagiarism.* Suggestions to help you maintain academic honesty, with illustrative examples.

- *Style Guide.* A brief guide to help you follow either MLA or Chicago Manual styles in citing your sources. The Modern Language Association style is widely used for papers in English composition, literature, and foreign languages. History, the fine arts, and some fields in the humanities (but not literature) use traditional footnotes or endnotes, which should conform to standards set by *The Chicago Manual of Style.*

We invite you to explore!

Contents

The Historical Legacies
of
Christopher Columbus

Kenneth J. Andrien

INTRODUCTION

Few historical figures have generated as much controversy over the last five hundred years as Christopher Columbus. For some he remains a heroic figure, advancing the frontiers of western civilization. For others his voyages are responsible for the ultimate deaths of millions of indigenous peoples and the destruction of the landscape that prevailed in the Americas before 1492. Despite the controversies surrounding his historical place in American and world history, Christopher Columbus remains an enigmatic figure. He left few documents for historians to analyze; even his journal of the first voyage was lost in the sixteenth century. From the scanty historical record, however, it seems clear that Columbus never really comprehended the consequences of his historic voyages, maintaining stubbornly to his death that he had reached Asia, not "discovered" a New World. From his return to Europe in 1493, his contemporaries also expressed widely divergent views about the man and his importance. These divisions have endured over time, so that modern historians most often speak of the multiple historical legacies of Christopher Columbus. Regardless of whether he is viewed as a hero or a villain, it is clear that his voyages began the process of global interdependency that characterizes our own modern world.

MODERN ASSESSMENTS OF CHRISTOPHER COLUMBUS

Modern scholarly works have expressed fundamental disagreements about the historical role and importance of Christopher Columbus. In most cases these differing interpretations of Columbus do not reflect new documentary discoveries about the life and times of the explorer. Instead, they tend to be influenced by the way the historical figure of Columbus fits into the scholarly and political currents of the historians' own times. This was particularly apparent in the quincentennary of the Columbian voyages in 1992, when various groups within the United States—such as Amerindians, environmentalists, Latinos, Italian Americans, and members of the scholarly community—all expressed widely divergent views about the historical legacies of the man. This has also proven true of virtually every historical period since the results of the first voyage of Columbus became public. For students of history, the "simple" construction and interpretation of the past is a very complex and difficult problem.

Christopher Columbus and the Spread of Western Civilization

Samuel Eliot Morison's biography of Christopher Columbus, published in 1942, emphasized the explorer's heroic efforts to advance western civilization. For Morison, Columbus was a daring mariner and a visionary, who served as an inspiration to a beleaguered United States during World War II and provided hope for the future. The following excerpt is taken from Samuel Eliot Morison, Admiral of the Ocean Sea: A Life of Christopher Columbus *(reprint edition, Philadelphia, 1978),* 673–75.

America would eventually have been discovered if the Great Enterprise of Columbus had been rejected; yet who can predict what would have been the outcome? The voyage that took him to "The Indies" and home was no blind chance, but the creation of his own brain and soul, long studied, carefully planned, repeatedly urged on indifferent princes, and carried through by virtue of his courage, sea-knowledge and indomitable will. No later voyage could ever have such spectacular results, and Columbus's fame would have been secure had he retired from the sea in 1493. Yet a lofty ambition to explore further, to organize the territories won for Castile, and to complete the circuit of the globe, sent him thrice more to America. These voyages, even more than the first, proved him to be the greatest navigator of his age, and enabled him to train the captains and pilots who were to display the banners of Spain off every American cape and island between Fifty North and Fifty South. The ease with which he dissipated the unknown terrors of the Ocean, the skill with which he found his way out and home, again and again, led thousands of men from every Western European nation into maritime adventure and exploration. And if Columbus was a failure as a colonial administrator, it was partly because his conception of a colony transcended the desire of his followers to impart, and the capacity of natives to receive, the institutions and culture of Renaissance Europe.

Columbus had a proud, passionate and sensitive nature that suffered deeply from the contempt to which he was early subjected, and the envy, disloyalty, ingratitude and injustice which he met as a discoverer. He wrote so freely out of the abundance of his complaint, as to give the impression that his life was more full of woe than of weal. That impression is false. As with other mari-

Christopher Columbus (1451–1506), navigator and explorer.

ners, a month at sea healed the wounds of a year ashore, and a fair wind blew away the memory of foul weather. Command of a tall and gallant ship speeding over blue water before a fresh trade wind, shaping her course for some new and marvelous land where gold is abundant and the women are kind, is a mariner's dream of the good life. Columbus had a Hellenic sense of wonder at the new and strange, combined with an artist's appreciation of natural beauty; and his voyages to this strange new world brought him to some of the most gorgeous coastlines on the earth's surface. Moreover, Columbus had a deep conviction of the immanence, the sovereignty and the infinite wisdom of God, which transcended all his suffering, and enhanced all his triumphs. Waste no pity on the Admiral of the Ocean Sea! He enjoyed long stretches of pure delight such as only a seaman may know, and moments of high, proud exultation that only a discoverer can experience.

One only wishes that the Admiral might have been afforded the sense of fulfillment that would have come from foreseeing all that flowed from his discoveries; that would have turned all the sorrows of his last years to joy. The whole history of the Americas stems from the Four Voyages of Columbus; and as the Greek city-states looked back to the deathless gods as their founders, so today a score of independent nations and dominions unite in homage to Christopher the stout-hearted son of Genoa, who carried Christian civilization across the Ocean Sea.

Christopher Columbus and the Legacy of Colonial Brutality

In his classic study of the Spanish Caribbean, Carl Ortwin Sauer presents a very different image of Christopher Columbus than Morison's. For Sauer, Columbus was a romantic self-promoter, who never truly understood the significance of his discoveries. Moreover, he proved a poor leader and a ruthless administrator; his lust for profits led him to promote a legacy of exploitation and brutality that characterized much of the early European expansion into the New World. The following passage is taken from Carl Ortwin Sauer, The Early Spanish Main *(Berkeley, 1966), 290–91, 104, 291.*

Columbus had a genius for words, not as to their proper meaning but to cast a spell and to persuade. Soon after getting to Haiti he decided to name it "the Spanish Isle." One of its valleys earliest seen became the Valle del Paraiso. Other parts were likened to the fairest parts of Andalusia in spring. The silvery cloud-capped crest of a northern ridge gave name to Puerto Plata. The outlet of the Gulf of Paria was the Dragon's Mouth. Carib islands took the name of the shrines of Guadelupe and Montserrat. The romantic publicity he gave to the new lands above all was to portray them as lands of infinite gold. All the fabled gold lands of antiquity were relocated in his discoveries or in parts he was about to discover. Columbus was looking for gold mines from the first landing on a coral island to his last days in Veragua. It did not matter that his success was slight. Always and everywhere there was vast promise of gold. The sovereigns and people of Spain became imbued by his obsession, picturesquely and fantastically presented. The course of Spanish empire was first turned to its fateful search for gold by the *idée fixe* that dominated Columbus. . . .

The seven years of Columbus' government were a continuing and growing series of disappointments and deficits. The extravagant prospectuses of promised wealth went on but revenues did

Reprinted from *The Early Spanish Main* by Carl Ortwin Sauer. Published by the University of California Press, 1966. Copyright © 1966 by The Regents of the University of California.

not materialize. When gold was not forthcoming, Columbus attributed it to a temporary withholding of divine favor and would bridge the interval by the easy and sure profits of dyewood and slaves, for which he presented wholly imaginary figures. As he continued to hold to an illusory geography undisturbed by every evidence that he was wrong, so he invented riches that did not exist. It was well apparent that he was a chronic, compulsive romancer who lived in a world of wishful thinking.

Nor did Columbus know how to govern men. He failed signally in getting men to follow him faithfully. . . . There had been no time of peace and goodwill. . . . Columbus lacked ability and inclination to adapt himself and to learn from changing circumstances. He had secured an excessive title to which he clung. These were his Indies over which his rule would be absolute and which he would pass on to his heirs. . . .

His Indian policy was simple, rigid, and unworkable. He found the natives friendly, apt at learning, and timorous. He would put them to work to produce gold, which their caciques would collect on a per capita basis. The impossible demand turned amiability to fear, flight, and retaliation. Many were captured, more died of hunger. Caciques were liquidated, their subjects shipped as slaves. Pacification by terror began thus as an instrument of colonial policy.

The government of Columbus was a continuing series of bad decisions. Always he insisted that he had been right and would have succeeded but for his enemies. Experience taught him nothing. The heritage of his mistakes continued long after him.

Columbus and the Ecological "Revolution"

The prominent historian Alfred Crosby expresses another negative assessment of the Columbian voyages, emphasizing the massive ecological and social changes following 1492. Although Crosby virtually ignores the historical figure of Columbus, he provides a measured scholarly discussion of the interchange of plants, animals, and biota between the Americas and the rest of the world. It was an exchange, however, that Crosby ultimately finds had negative consequences for the modern world. The selection is taken from Alfred W. Crosby, Jr., The Colum-

bian Exchange: Biological and Cultural Consequences of 1492
(*Westport, Connecticut, 1972*), 218–19.

The long-range biological effects of the Columbian exchange
are not encouraging.

If one values all forms of life and not just the life of one's own
species, then one must be concerned with the genetic pool, the
total potential of all living things to produce descendants of various shapes, sizes, colors, internal structures, defenses against both
multicellular and unicellular enemies, maximum fertility, and, to
speak generally, maximum ability to produce offspring with
maximum adaptive possibilities. The genetic pool is usually expanded when continents join. As plants and creatures move into
virgin territory, the adaptations to new environments of those
who survive the increased competition produce new types and
even many new species. Paleontologists and comparative zoolo-
gists call the event "explosive evolution," meaning that it often
only takes a few million years. This is what normally would have
happened and would be happening after the joining of the Old
and New Worlds in 1492—but for man.

Not for half a billion years, at least, and probably for long
before that, has an extreme or permanent physical change affected
the whole earth. The single exception to this generality may be
European man and his technologies, agricultural and industrial.
He has spread all over the globe, and non-European peoples have
adopted his techniques in all but the smallest islets. His effect is
comparable to an increase in the influx of cosmic rays or the
raising of whole new chains of Andes and Himalayas.

The Columbian exchange has included man, and he has
changed the Old and New Worlds sometimes inadvertently,
sometimes intentionally, often brutally. It is possible that he and
the plants and animals he brings with him have caused the extinc-
tion of more species of life forms in the last four hundred years
than the usual processes of evolution might kill off in a million.
Man kills faster than the pace of evolution: there has been no
million years since Columbus for evolution to devise a replace-
ment for the passenger pigeon. No one can remember what the
pre-Columbian flora of the Antilles was like, and the trumpeter

---

Reprinted from *The Columbian Exchange: Biological and Cultural Consequences of 1492* by Alfred W. Crosby, Jr. Published by Greenwood Press,
Inc., 1972. Copyright © 1972 by Alfred W. Crosby, Jr.

swan and the buffalo and a hundred other species have been reduced to such small numbers that a mere twitch of a change in ecology or man's wishes can eliminate them. The flora and fauna of the Old and especially of the New World have been reduced and specialized by man. Specialization almost always narrows the possibilities for future changes: for the sake of present convenience, we loot the future.

The Columbian exchange has left us with not a richer but a more impoverished genetic pool. We, all of the life on this planet, are the less for Columbus, and the impoverishment will increase.

Columbus and the Advent of Global Interdependency

In the following assessment, the authors seek to place Christopher Columbus in his historical context. They stress that Columbus unconsciously initiated the "modern" era of global interdependency, with all of its positive and negative consequences. Taken from William D. Phillips, Jr., and Carla Rahn Phillips, The Worlds of Christopher Columbus *(Cambridge, England, 1992), 241, 272–73.*

THE POST-COLUMBIAN WORLD is, of course, the modern world. Its increasingly interdependent and interconnected societies began to be linked together in the late fifteenth century, following Spanish voyages to the west and Portuguese voyages southward and eastward to Asia. After those early voyages, there has never been a time when the major civilizations of the world have lost contact with one another, never a time when major events could have only local consequences. From the diverse and isolated worlds on the face of the earth in the late Middle Ages, a single world has been woven together by merchants and missionaries, colonists and conquerers, imperialists and idealists. Columbus placed the world on the path leading toward global interdependence, with enormous consequences—both good and ill—for the peoples of the world. . . .

All of these changes—in government, society, plants, animals, money, and trade—evolved in the aftermath of the voyages of Christopher Columbus. Yet we should take care not to attribute the changes solely to those voyages or to assume that they would not have occurred without him. Enormous changes in human history can rarely be attributed to one person or one set of events. Instead, we should try to view the voyages of Columbus as the culmination of one scene in a much broader drama. If Columbus had not sailed westward in search of Asia, someone else would soon have done so. The time was right for such a bold undertaking, and the European economy was poised to take advantage of the expanded trade that a direct ocean route to Asia would afford.

Yet Columbus was clearly well positioned for the role that history assigned him. Experienced with trade and with the sea, widely read in the cosmography of the day, and fortuitously given the opportunity to benefit from the best contemporary geographical knowledge, he was the right man in the right place at the right time. That, and his strength of character and perseverance, justly earned him the fame that he still enjoys, five hundred years after his first historic voyage. Columbus believed that great changes would transform the world as a result of his voyages: the conversion of all peoples to Christianity, the creation of a single world empire, and the Second Coming of Christ that would end world history altogether in the Last Judgment of humanity. The changes that actually occurred seem rather tame in comparison with the Apocalypse, yet they were profound enough to shape the modern world.

Questions

---

1. *What do you think were the principal positive achievements of Christopher Columbus? What were the negative consequences?*
2. *How important was Christopher Columbus in the historical events that have transpired since 1492? Was he a heroic figure or a villain?*

3. *How important is Christopher Columbus in shaping the history of the United States? What was his role in world history? Are they the same or different?*
4. *To what extent does the legacy of the Columbian voyages still shape our own lives? Why do you think Christopher Columbus remains such a controversial figure? How do you assess the positive and negative consequences of his life on history?*

COLUMBUS'S LEGACY IN THE DOCUMENTARY RECORD

The principal documentary source about the first voyage of Christopher Columbus is his journal or logbook, intended to inform the monarchs of Castile about his journey. In this work, Columbus often focused on what might have pleased the crown, rather than simply recording events. In addition, it is clear that Columbus did not always understand the ecological, human, and geographical landscape that he encountered. An even more serious problem with interpreting the journal, however, is that all of the original copies were lost sometime in the sixteenth century. The only remaining copy is a transcription of the original made in the 1550s by the Dominican friar, Bartolomé de las Casas, who used it as a source in writing his Historia de las Indias. *Las Casas, a vigorous champion of the Amerindians, introduced his own biases, made numerous copying errors, often summarized or omitted points, and even interjected his own comments. The result is a primary source that must be used very carefully by any student of the period.*

The only original documentary record of the first voyage is the 1493 letter of Columbus, but this document too has its limitations. It reads like an advertising brochure designed to encourage future investments in a second voyage of Columbus to the New World.

The remaining documents in this collection deal with the wide impact of the Columbian voyages on the course of world history. Nevertheless, they too contain exaggerations, reflecting the biases of their authors and the limited abilities of contemporaries to understand the magnitude of the changes affecting their lives.

The Journal of Christopher Columbus

The document that follows serves as the introduction to the journal of Columbus. It recounts how the monarchs of "the Spains" agreed to support Columbus after their formal conquest of the Muslim city of Granada in 1492, followed by the expulsion of the Jews from the country shortly afterward.[1] Columbus links his own voyage to the monarch's "triumphs" by promising to spread the Christian faith after his arrival in Asia. He also reminds them of the many titles granted to his family and promises to record his voyage faithfully in the ensuing journal. This selection is taken from The Journal of Christopher Columbus, *trans. Cecil Jane (London, 1968), 3–4, 6.*

Journal Introduction

Most Christian and most exalted and most excellent and most mighty princes, King and Queen of the Spains and of the islands of the sea, our Sovereigns: Forasmuch as, in this present year of 1492, after that Your Highnesses had made an end of the war with the Moors who reigned in Europe, and had brought that war to a conclusion in the very great city of Granada, . . . and afterwards in that same month, on the ground of information which I had given to Your Highnesses concerning the lands of India, and concerning a prince who is called 'Grand Khan,' which is to say in our Romance tongue 'King of Kings,' how many times he and his ancestors had sent to Rome to beg for men learned in our holy faith, in order that they might instruct him therein, and how the Holy Father had never made provision in this matter, and how so many nations had been lost, falling into idolatries and taking to themselves doctrines of perdition, and Your Highnesses, as Catholic Christians and as princes devoted to the holy Christian

---

[1] Spain was not a nation-state in 1492; it was united when Ferdinand of Aragon and Isabel of Castile married in 1469 and ascended their respective thrones ten years later. Thus, it was merely a dynastic union, and the institutions of both kingdoms remained separate. Columbus recognizes this tenuous unity by referring to Ferdinand and Isabel as monarchs of the "Spains."

Reprinted from *The Journal of Christopher Columbus*, Cecil Jane, Translator. Published by Anthony Blond Ltd., London, 1968. Copyright © 1965 by Clarkson N. Potter Inc.

faith and propagators thereof, and enemies of the sect of Mahomet and of all idolatries and heresies, took thought to send me, Christopher Columbus, to the said parts of India, to see those princes and peoples and lands and the character of them and of all else, and the manner which should be used to bring about their conversion to our holy faith, and ordained that I should not go by land to the eastward, by which way it was the custom to go, but by way of the west, by which down to this day we do not know certainly that any one has passed; therefore, after having driven out all the Jews from your realms and lordships, in the same month of January, Your Highnesses commanded me that, with a sufficient fleet, I should go to the said parts of India and for this accorded to me great rewards and ennobled me so that from that time henceforward I might style myself 'don' and be high admiral of the Ocean Sea and viceroy and perpetual governor of the islands and continent which I should discover and gain and which from now henceforward might be discovered and gained in the Ocean Sea, and that my eldest son should succeed to the same position, and so on from generation to generation. And I departed from the city of Granada on the twelfth day of the month of May in the same year of 1492, on a Saturday, and came to the town of Palos, which is a port of the sea, where I made ready three ships, very suited for such an undertaking, and I set out from that port, well furnished with very many supplies and with many seamen, on the third day of the month of August of the same year, on a Friday, half an hour before the rising of the sun, and I steered my course for the Canary Islands of Your Highnesses, which are in the Ocean Sea, thence to set out on my way and to sail until I should arrive in the Indies, and deliver the embassy of Your Highnesses to those princes and perform all that you had commanded me to do. To this end, I thought to write all this journey very carefully, from day to day, all that I might do and see and experience, as will be hereafter seen.

The next journal entry records the first landfall of the voyage and the initial encounter with the indigenous peoples of the Caribbean. Columbus dutifully claimed the lands for his sovereigns and noted the good relations that developed between his crew members and the inhabitants of the islands. He obviously viewed the Amerindians as human beings but as technologically inferior. Columbus also alluded to the apparent animosity that existed between these people and their neighbors, who sought to enslave them. Notice how Las Casas interposes himself into the narrative at various places. This excerpt is taken from The Journal of Christopher Columbus, 22–24.

Thursday, October 11th/[12th]

He navigated to the west-south-west; . . . Two hours after midnight land appeared, at a distance of about two leagues from them. They took in all sail, remaining with the mainsail, which is the great sail without bonnets, and kept jogging, waiting for day, a Friday, on which they reached a small island of the Lucayos, which is called in the language of the Indians "Guanahaní." Immediately they saw naked people, and the admiral went ashore in the armed boat, and Martin Alonso Pinzón and Vicente Yañez, his brother, who was captain of the *Niña*. The admiral brought out the royal standard, and . . . [w]hen they had landed, they saw very green trees and much water and fruit of various kinds. The admiral called the two captains and the others who had landed, and Rodrigo de Escobedo, secretary of the whole fleet, and Rodrigo Sanchez de Segovia, and said that they should bear witness and testimony how he, before them all, took possession of the island, as in fact he did, for the King and Queen, his Sovereigns, making

A seventeenth-century engraving, showing newly discovered America as a paradise.

the declarations which are required, as is contained more at length in the testimonies which were there made in writing. Soon many people of the island gathered there. What follows are the actual words of the admiral, in his book of his first voyage and discovery of these Indies.

"I," he says, "in order that they might feel great amity towards us, because I knew that they were a people to be delivered and converted to our holy faith rather by love than by force, gave to some among them some red caps and some glass beads, which they hung round their necks, and many other things of little value. At this they were greatly pleased and became so entirely our friends that it was a wonder to see. Afterwards they came swimming to the ships' boats, where we were, and brought us parrots and cotton thread in balls, and spears and many other things, and we exchanged for them other things, such as small glass beads and hawks' bells, which we gave to them. In fact, they took all and gave all, such as they had, with good will, but it seemed to me that they were a people very deficient in everything. They all go naked as their mothers bore them, and the women also, although I saw only one very young girl. And all those whom I did see were youths, so that I did not see one who was over thirty years of age; they were very well built, with very handsome bodies and very good faces. Their hair is coarse almost like the hairs of a horse's tail and short; they wear their hair down over their eyebrows, except for a few strands behind, which they wear long and never cut. Some of them are painted black, and they are the colour of the people of the Canaries, neither black nor white, and some of them are painted white and some red and some in any colour that they find. Some of them paint their faces, some their whole bodies, some only the eyes, and some only the nose. They do not bear arms or know them, for I showed to them swords and they took them by the blade and cut themselves through ignorance. They have no iron. Their spears are certain reeds, without iron, and some of these have a fish tooth at the end, while others are pointed in various ways. They are all generally fairly tall, good looking and well proportioned. I saw some who bore marks of wounds on their bodies, and I made signs to them to ask how this came about, and they indicated to me that people came from other islands, which are near, and wished to capture them, and they defended themselves. And I believed and still believe that they come here from the mainland to take them for slaves. They should be good servants and of quick intelligence, since I see that they very soon say all that is said to them, and I believe that they would easily be made Christians, for it appeared to me that they had no creed. Our Lord willing, at the time of my departure I will bring back six of them to Your Highnesses, that they may learn to talk. I saw no beast of any kind in this island, except parrots." All these are the words of the admiral.

The journal returns to the theme of warfare among the indigenous peoples by introducing the Caribs, who are pictured as cannibals. These entries are very controversial among historians because the supporting evidence for cannibalism or even the existence of a separate Carib people is very scanty. Some scholars believe that Columbus introduced these passages to justify the violent skirmishes that broke out between his men and indigenous groups. Others even speculate that these references to cannibalism, which Europeans considered a particularly inhumane or "barbaric" practice, were merely excuses for the subjugation of these indigenous peoples. The passage is taken from The Journal of Christopher Columbus, 146–48.

Sunday, January 13th

He sent the boat to land at a beautiful beach, in order that they might take *ajes* [edible tropical plants] to eat, and they found some men with bows and arrows, with whom they paused to talk, and they bought two bows and many arrows, and asked one of them to go to speak with the admiral in the caravel, and he came. The admiral says that he was more ugly in appearance than any whom he had seen. He had his face all stained with charcoal, although in all other parts they are accustomed to paint themselves with various colours; he wore all his hair very long and drawn back and tied behind, and then gathered in meshes of parrots' feathers, and he was as naked as the others. The admiral judged that he must be one of the Caribs who eat men and that the gulf, which he had seen yesterday, divided the land and that it must be an island by itself. He questioned him concerning the Caribs, and the Indian indicated to him that they were near there to the east, and the admiral says that he sighted this land yesterday before he entered that bay. The Indian told him that in that land there was much gold, and pointing to the poop of the caravel, which was very large, said that there were pieces of that size. He called gold "tuob," and did not understand it by "caona," as they call it in the first part of the island, or by "nozay," as they name it in San Salvador and in the other islands. . . . The admiral says further that in the islands which he had passed they were in great terror of Carib: in some islands they call it "Caniba," but in Española "Carib"; and they must be a daring people, since they go through all the islands and eat the people they can take. He says that he understood some words, and from them he says that he gathered other things, and the Indians whom he carried with him understood more, although they found a difference of languages, owing to the great distance between the lands. He ordered food to be given to the Indian, and gave him pieces of green and red cloth, and glass beads, to which they are very much attached, and sent him back to shore. And he told him to bring him gold, if there was any, which he believed to be the case from certain small ornaments which he was wearing. When the boat reached the shore, there were behind the trees quite fifty-five men, naked, with very long hair, as women wear their hair in Castile. At the back of the head, they wore tufts of parrot feathers and feathers of other birds, and each one carried his bow. The Indian landed and caused the others to lay aside their bows and arrows and a short stick, . . . which they carry in place of a sword. Afterwards they came to the boat and the people from the boat landed, and they began to buy from them their bows and arrows and other weapons, because the admiral had ordered this to be done. When two bows had been sold, they would not give more, but prepared rather to assault the Christians and capture them. They went running to collect their bows and arrows, where they had laid them aside, and came back with ropes in their hands, in order, as he says, to bind the Christians. Seeing them come running towards them, the Christians, being on guard, as the admiral always advised them to be, fell upon them, and they gave an Indian a great slash on the buttocks and they wounded another in the breast with an arrow. When they saw that they could gain little, although the Christians were not more than seven and they were fifty and more, they turned in flight, so that not one remained, one leaving his arrows here and another his bow there. The Christians, as he says, would have killed many of them, if the pilot who went with them as their captain had not prevented it.

The Letter of Columbus to Ferdinand and Isabel

The following excerpt from the letter of Christopher Columbus to King Ferdinand and Queen Isabel was undoubtedly intended to publicize the successes of the first voyage. The size and potential richness of the islands are apparently exaggerated to impress the monarchs (and any other potential investors) and generate support for any future voyages by Columbus. Although he scarcely refers to the Caribs, Columbus does emphasize the exotic qualities of the newly discovered lands, particularly the nudity of the inhabitants. Apart from illustrating the "primitive" social system of the native peoples, these references were probably also meant to evoke (in the reading audience) an image of the biblical Garden of Eden. This copy of the letter may be found in The Journal of Christopher Columbus, *191, 194, 196–98, 200–201.*

SIR: Since I know that you will be pleased at the great victory with which Our Lord has crowned my voyage, I write this to you, from which you will learn how in thirty-three days I passed from the Canary Islands to the Indies, with the fleet which the most illustrious King and Queen, our Sovereigns, gave to me. There I found very many islands, filled with innumerable people, and I have taken possession of them all for their Highnesses, done by proclamation and with the royal standard unfurled, and no opposition was offered to me.

To the first island which I found I gave the name "San Salvador," in remembrance of the Divine Majesty, Who had marvellously bestowed all this; the Indians call it "Guanahani." To the second, I gave the name the island of "Santa Maria de Concepcion," to the third, "Fernandina," to the fourth, "Isabella," to the fifth island, "Juana," and so each received from me a new name. . . .

Española is a marvel. The sierras and the mountains, the plains, the champaigns, are so lovely and so rich for planting and sowing, for breeding cattle of every kind, for building towns and villages. The harbours of the sea here are such as cannot be believed to exist unless they have been seen, and so with the rivers, many and great, and of good water, the majority of which contain gold. In the trees, fruits and plants, there is a great difference from those of Juana. In this island, there are many spices and great mines of gold and of other metals.

The people of this island and of all the other islands which I have found and of which I have information, all go naked, men and women, as their mothers bore them, although some of the women cover a single place with the leaf of a plant or with a net of cotton which they make for the purpose. They have no iron or steel or weapons, nor are they fitted to use them. This is not because they are not well built and of handsome stature, but because they are very marvellously timorous. They have no other arms than spears made of canes, cut in seeding time, to the ends of which they fix a small sharpened stick. Of these they do not dare to make use, for many times it has happened that I have sent ashore two or three men to some town to have speech with them, and countless people have come out to them, and as soon as they have seen my men approaching, they have fled, a father not even waiting for his son. This is not because ill has been done to any one of them; on the contrary, at every place where I have been and have been able to have speech with them, I have given to them of that which I had, such as cloth and many other things, receiving

Native Americans congregate as ships arrive from the New World in this German woodcut.

nothing in exchange. But so they are, incurably timid. It is true that, after they have been reassured and have lost this fear, they are so guileless and so generous with all that they possess, that no one would believe it who has not seen it. They refuse nothing that they possess, if it be asked of them; on the contrary, they invite any one to share it and display as much love as if they would give their hearts. They are content with whatever trifle of whatever kind that may be given to them, whether it be of value or valueless. I forbade that they should be given things so worthless as fragments of broken crockery, scraps of broken glass and lace tips, although when they were able to get them, they fancied that they possessed the best jewel in the world. So it was found that for a thong a sailor received gold to the weight of two and a half castellanos, and others received much more for other things which were worth less. As for new blancas, for them they would give everything which they had, although it might be two or three castellanos' [gold coins] weight of gold or an arroba or two of spun cotton. They took even the pieces of the broken hoops of the wine barrels and, like savages, gave what they had, so that it seemed to me to be wrong and I forbade it. I gave them a thousand handsome good things, which I had brought, in order that they might conceive affection for us and, more than that, might become Christians and be inclined to the love and service of Your Highnesses and of the whole Castilian nation, and strive to collect and give us of the things which they have in abundance and which are necessary to us.

They do not hold any creed nor are they idolaters; but they all believe that power and good are in the heavens and were very firmly convinced that I, with these ships and men, came from the heavens, and in this belief they everywhere received me after they had mastered their fear. This belief is not the result of ignorance, for they are, on the contrary, of a very acute intelligence and they are men who navigate all those seas, so that it is amazing how good an account they give of everything. It is because they have never seen people clothed or ships of such a kind.

As soon as I arrived in the Indies, in the first island which I found, I took some of the natives by force, in order that they might learn and might give me information of whatever there is in these parts. And so it was that they soon understood us, and we them, either by speech or signs, and they have been very serviceable. At present, those I bring with me are still of the opinion that I come from Heaven, for all the intercourse which they have had with me. They were the first to announce this wherever I went, and the others went running from house to house, and to the neighbouring towns, with loud cries of, "Come! Come! See the men from Heaven!" So all came, men and women alike, when their minds were set at rest concerning us, not one, small or great, remaining behind, and they all brought something to eat and drink, which they gave with extraordinary affection. . . .

In all these islands, I saw no great diversity in the appearance of the people or in their manners and language. On the contrary, they all understand one another, which is a very curious thing, on account of which I hope that their Highnesses will determine upon their conversion to our holy faith, towards which they are very inclined.

I have already said how I went one hundred and seven leagues in a straight line from west to east along the seashore of the island of Juana, and as a result of this voyage I can say that this island is larger than England and Scotland together, for, beyond these one hundred and seven leagues, there remain to the westward two provinces to which I have not gone. One of these provinces they call "Avan," and there people are born with tails. These provinces cannot have a length of less than fifty or sixty leagues, as I could understand from those Indians whom I have and who know all the islands.

The other island, Española, has a circumference greater than all Spain from Collioure by the seacoast to Fuenterabia in Vizcaya, for I voyaged along one side for one hundred and eighty-eight great leagues in a straight line from west to east. It is a land to be desired and, when seen, never to be left. I have taken possession of all for their Highnesses, and all are more richly endowed than I know how or am able to say, and I hold all for their Highnesses, so that they may dispose of them as they do of the kingdoms of Castile and as absolutely. But especially, in this Española, in the situation most convenient and in the best position for the mines of gold and for all trade as well with the mainland here as with that there, belonging to the Grand Khan, where will be great trade and profit, I have taken possession of a large town, to which I gave the name "Villa de Navidad," and in it I have made fortifications and a fort, which will now by this time be entirely completed. In it I have left enough men for such a purpose with arms and artillery and provisions for more than a year, and a fusta, and one, a master of all seacraft, to build others, and I have established great friend-ship with the king of that land, so much so, that he was proud to call me "brother" and to treat me as such. . . .

In conclusion, to speak only of what has been accomplished on this voyage, which was so hasty, their Highnesses can see that I will give them as much gold as they may need, if their Highnesses will render me very slight assistance; presently, I will give them spices and cotton, as much as their Highnesses shall command; and mastic, as much as they shall order to be shipped and which, up to now, has been found only in Greece, in the island of Chios, and the Seignory sells it for what it pleases; and aloe, as much as they shall order to be shipped; and slaves, as many as they shall order, and who will be from the idolaters. I believe also that I have found rhubarb and cinnamon, and I shall find a thou-sand other things of value, which the people whom I have left there will have discovered, for I have not delayed at any point, so far as the wind allowed me to sail, except in the town of Navidad, in order to leave it secured and well established, and in truth I should have done much more if the ships had served me as reason demanded. . . .

This is an account of the facts, thus abridged.

Done in the caravel, off the Canary Islands, on the fifteenth day of February, in the year one thousand four hundred and ninety-three.

The Amerindians and the "Garden of Eden"

The attempt to picture the Amerindians as an innocent and childlike race, so apparent in the Columbus letter, was a common theme in the sixteenth century. Members of the clergy often used this image to prove that the indigenous peoples were "real" human beings (rather than some form of savage animals), to protect them from exploitation from the settlers, and also to gain control over their conversion to Christianity from rival clerical or lay organizations. The following passage is filled with language meant to evoke an image of the Garden of Eden, not the realities of Amerindian life in the Americas. The passage is taken from Bartolomé de las Casas, Very Brief Account of the Destruction of the Indies, *trans. Francis Augustus MacNutt in* Bartholomew De Las

Casas: His Life, His Apostolate, and His Writings *(New York, 1909)*, 314–15.

God has created all these numberless people to be quite the simplest, without malice or duplicity, most obedient, most faithful to their natural Lords, and to the Christians, whom they serve; the most humble, most patient, most peaceful, and calm, without strife nor tumults; not wrangling, nor querulous, as free from uproar, hate and desire of revenge, as any in the world.

They are likewise the most delicate people, weak and of feeble constitution, and less than any other can they bear fatigue, and they very easily die of whatsoever infirmity; so much so, that not even the sons of our Princes and of nobles, brought up in royal and gentle life, are more delicate than they; although there are among them such as are of the peasant class. They are also a very poor people, who of worldly goods possess little, nor wish to possess: and they are therefore neither proud, nor ambitious, nor avaricious. . . .

They are likewise of a clean, unspoiled, and vivacious intellect, very capable, and receptive to every good doctrine; most prompt to accept our Holy Catholic Faith, to be endowed with virtuous customs; and they have as little difficulty with such things as any people created by God in the world.

Once they have begun to learn of matters pertaining to faith, they are so importunate to know them, and in frequenting the sacraments and divine service of the Church, that to tell the truth, the clergy have need to be endowed of God with the gift of pre-eminent patience to bear with them: and finally, I have heard many lay Spaniards frequently say many years ago, (unable to deny the goodness of those they saw) certainly these people were the most blessed of the earth, had they only knowledge of God.

The "Sins" of the Spanish Invasion

Militant friars like Las Casas and many of his fellow Dominicans also tried to picture the Spanish conquistadors and settlers as vicious and cruel exploiters. These tales had some basis in reality, but they were also

Bartolome de Las Casas, (1474–1566), missionary leader.

aimed at convincing a European audience that the excesses of the conquest had to be curbed and the powers of the crown and the clergy expanded in the New World. Along with the images of the indigenous peoples as innocents reminiscent of the Garden of Eden, they created a powerful picture of European excesses. According to many friars, these abuses undermined the chances for salvation of all Christians who tolerated such "sins" against humanity. The selection below is taken from Bartolomé de las Casas, Very Brief Account of the Destruction of the Indies, trans. Francis Augustus MacNutt in Bartholomew De Las Casas, 319–20.

The Christians, with their horses and swords and lances, began to slaughter and practise strange cruelty among them. They penetrated into the country and spared neither children nor the aged, nor pregnant women, nor those in child labour, all of whom they ran through the body and lacerated, as though they were assaulting so many lambs herded in their sheepfold.

They made bets as to who would slit a man in two, or cut off his head at one blow: or they opened up his bowels. They tore the babes from their mothers' breast by the feet, and dashed their heads against the rocks. Others they seized by the shoulders and threw into the rivers, laughing and joking, and when they fell into the water they exclaimed: "boil body of so and so!" They spitted the bodies of other babes, together with their mothers and all who were before them, on their swords.

They made a gallows just high enough for the feet to nearly touch the ground, and by thirteens, in honour and reverence of our Redeemer and the twelve Apostles, they put wood underneath and, with fire, they burned the Indians alive. . . .

And because all the people who could flee, hid among the mountains and climbed the crags to escape from men so deprived of humanity, so wicked, such wild beasts, exterminators and capital enemies of all the human race, the Spaniards taught and trained the fiercest boar-hounds to tear an Indian to pieces as soon as they saw him, so that they more willingly attacked and ate one, than if he had been a boar. These hounds made great havoc and slaughter.

The Onset of the Epidemics

The introduction of European diseases brought unprecedented devastation upon the Amerindian peoples. In Mexico, for example, some historical demographers estimate the precontact Amerindian population at 20-25 million; within one hundred years that number had fallen to 1.5 million, largely as a result of epidemic diseases. Often the epidemics arrived even before the Spanish forces, spread by indigenous peoples who had contact with the Europeans. The following passage, taken from an indigenous (Aztec) source recounts the devastation of a smallpox epidemic in the valley of Mexico, which preceded the arrival of the Spaniards, weakened the indigenous peoples, and paved the way for the conquistadores' ultimate victories. This excerpt is taken from Fray Bernardino de Sahagún, Florentine Codex: General History of the Things of New Spain, *trans. Arthur J. O. Anderson and Charles E. Dibble (Santa Fe, 1955), 12:81.*

And [even] before the Spaniards had risen against us, a pestilence first came to be prevalent: the smallpox. It was [the month of] Tepeilhuitl when it began, and it spread over the people as great destruction. Some it quite covered [with pustules] on all

From the *Florentine Codex: General History of the Things of New Spain* by Fray Bernardino de Sahagún. Arthur J. O. Anderson and Charles E. Dibble, Translators. Published by The School of American Research and The University of Utah, 1955.

parts—their faces, their heads, their breasts, etc. There was great havoc. Very many died of it. They could not walk; they only lay in their resting places and beds. They could not move; they could not stir; they could not change position, nor lie on one side, nor face down, nor on their backs. And if they stirred, much did they cry out. Great was its destruction. Covered, mantled with pustules, very many people died of them. And very many starved; there was death from hunger, [for] none could take care of [the sick]; nothing could be done for them.

And on some the pustules were widely separated; they suffered not greatly, neither did many [of them] die. Yet many people were marred by them on their faces; one's face or nose was pitted. Some lost their eyes; they were blinded.

At this time, this pestilence prevailed sixty days, sixty day signs. When it left, when it abated, when there was recovery and the return of life, the plague had already moved toward Chalco, whereby many were disabled—not, however, completely crippled. When it came to be prevalent, [it was the month of] Teotl eco. And when it went, weakened, it was Panquetzaliztli. Then the Mexicans, the chieftains, could revive.

And after this, then the Spaniards came.

Amerindians View the Spanish Invasion

For the highly advanced Amerindian civilizations, the arrival of the Europeans signaled a massive change in their religious, social, and economic way of life. Many Amerindians resisted these changes, clinging to their traditional ways and changing them as little as possible. The following passage from the Mayan peoples of Mesoamerica has a nostalgic quality, harkening back to better days before the Europeans arrived. It is taken from The Book of Chilam Balam of Chumayel, *trans. Ralph L. Roys (Norman, Oklahoma, 1967), 83.*

They did not wish to join with the foreigners; they did not desire Christianity. They did not wish to pay tribute, did those

Reprinted from *The Book of Chilam Balam of Chumayel*, Ralph L. Roys, Translator. Published by the Carnegie Institute of Washington, 1933. Copyright © 1967 by the University of Oklahoma Press.

whose emblems were the bird, the precious stone, the flat precious stone and the jaguar, those with the three magic <emblems>. Four-hundreds of years and fifteen score years was the end of their lives; then came the end of their lives, because they knew the measure of their days. Complete was the month; complete, the year; complete, the day; complete, the night; complete, the breath of life as it passed also; complete, the blood, when they arrived at their beds, their mats, their thrones. In due measure did they recite the good prayers; in due measure they sought the lucky days, until they saw the good stars enter into their reign; then they kept watch while the reign of the good stars began. Then everything was good.

Then they adhered to <the dictates of> their reason. There was no sin; in the holy faith their lives <were passed>. There was then no sickness; they had then no aching bones; they had then no high fever; they had then no smallpox; they had then no burning chest; they had then no abdominal pains; they had then no consumption; they had then no headache. At that time the course of humanity was orderly. The foreigners made it otherwise when they arrived here. They brought shameful things/when they came. They lost their innocence in carnal sin.

The Columbian Exchange

The first European explorers and settlers were often astounded by the rich and diverse plant and animal life, much of it unknown to them. Indeed, the concept of the Americas as a "New World" stemmed in part from the very different natural environment. As the passage below catalogs, the Americas had rich supplies of plant and animal life, which enriched the food supply of many parts of the world after 1492. Before the Columbian voyages, for example, Ireland had no potatoes, and commodities like corn or chocolate were unknown outside of the Western Hemisphere. Even the coca leaf was a traditional Andean crop. This passage is taken from José de Acosta, Historia natural y moral de las Indias *(Mexico City, 1940), in* Latin American Civilization: History and Society, 1492 to the Present, *ed. Benjamin Keen, 4th ed. (Boulder, 1986), 76–79.*

The Indians have their own words to signify bread, which in Peru is called *tanta* and in other parts is given other names. But the quality and substance of the bread the Indians use is very different from ours, for they have no kind of wheat, barley, millet, panic grass, or any grain such as is used in Europe to make bread. Instead they have other kinds of grains and roots, among which maize, called Indian wheat in Castile and Turkey grain in Italy, holds the first place. . . .

Maize is the Indian bread, and they commonly eat it boiled in the grain, hot, when it is called *mote* . . . ; sometimes they eat it toasted. There is a large and round maize, like that of the Lucanas, which the Spaniards eat as a delicacy; it has better flavor than toasted chickpeas. There is another and more pleasing way of preparing it, which consists in grinding the maize and making the flour into pancakes, which are put on the fire and later placed on the table and eaten piping hot; in some places they call them *arepas*. . . .

Maize is used by the Indians to make not only their bread but also their wine; from it they make beverages which produce drunkenness more quickly than wine made of grapes. They make this maize wine in various ways, calling it *azua* in Peru and more generally throughout the Indies *chicha*. The strongest sort is made like beer, steeping the grains of maize until they begin to break, after which they boil the juice in a certain way, which makes it so strong that a few drinks will produce intoxication. . . .

The cacao tree is most esteemed in Mexico and coca is favored in Peru; both trees are surrounded with considerable superstition. Cacao is a bean smaller and fattier than the almond, and when roasted has not a bad flavor. It is so much esteemed by the Indians, and even by the Spaniards, that it is the object of one of the richest and largest lines of trade of New Spain; since it is a dry fruit, and one that keeps a long time without spoiling, they send whole ships loaded with it from the province of Guatemala. Last year an English corsair burned in the port of Guatulco, in New Spain, more than one hundred thousand *cargas* of cacao. They also use it as money, for five cacao beans will buy one thing, thirty

Selections by José de Acosta, reprinted from *Latin American Civilization: History and Society, 1492 to the Present*, Fourth Edition, Benjamin Keen, editor, translator. Copyright © 1986 by WestviewPress. Reprinted by permission of WestviewPress.

another, and one hundred still another, and no objections are made to its use. They also use it as alms to give to the poor.

The chief use of this cacao is to make a drink that they call chocolate, which they greatly cherish in that country. But those who have not formed a taste for it dislike it, for it has a froth at the top and an effervescence like that formed in wine by dregs, so that one must really have great faith in it to tolerate it. In fine, it is the favorite drink of Indians and Spaniards alike, and they regale visitors to their country with it; the Spanish women of that land are particularly fond of the dark chocolate. They prepare it in various ways: hot, cold, and lukewarm. They usually put spices and much chili in it; they also make a paste of it, and they say that it is good for the chest and the stomach, and also for colds. Be that as it may, those who have not formed a taste for it do not like it. . . .

The cacao does not grow in Peru; instead they have the coca, which is surrounded with even greater superstition and really seems fabulous. In Potosí alone the commerce in coca amounts to more than 5,000,000 pesos, with a consumption of from 90 to 100,000 hampers, and in the year 1583 it was 100,000. . . . This coca that they so greatly cherish is a little green leaf which grows upon shrubs about one *estado* high. . . . It is commonly brought from the Andes, from valleys of insufferable heat, where it rains the greater part of the year, and it costs the Indians much labor and takes many lives, for they must leave their highlands and cold climates in order to cultivate it and carry it away. . . .

The Indians prize it beyond measure, and in the time of the Inca kings plebeians were forbidden to use coca without the permission of the Inca or his governor. Their custom is to hold it in their mouths, chewing and sucking it; they do not swallow it; they say that it gives them great strength and is a great comfort to them. Many serious men say that this is pure superstition and imagination. To tell the truth, I do not think so; I believe that it really does lend strength and endurance to the Indians, for one sees effects that cannot be attributed to imagination, such as their ability to journey two whole days on a handful of coca, eating nothing else, and similar feats.

Ecological Change

The Americas also underwent massive ecological changes brought about, in large part, by the introduction of European plant and animal life. The passage below provides some indication of the magnitude of these changes that followed the first Columbian voyages in 1492. The following document is also taken from José de Acosta, Historia natural y moral de las Indias *(Mexico City, 1940), in* Latin American Civilization: History and Society, 1492 to the Present, *ed. Benjamin Keen, 4th ed. (Boulder, 1986), 80–82.*

The Indies have been better repaid in the matter of plants than in any other kind of merchandise; for those few that have been carried from the Indies into Spain do badly there, whereas the many that have come over from Spain prosper in their new homes. I do not know whether to attribute this to the excellence of the plants that go from here or to the bounty of the soil over there. Nearly every good thing grown in Spain is found there; in some regions they do better than in others. They include wheat, barley, garden produce and greens and vegetables of all kinds, such as lettuce, cabbage, radishes, onions, garlic, parsley, turnips, carrots, eggplants, endive, salt-wort, spinach, chickpeas, beans, and lentils—in short, whatever grows well here, for those who have gone to the Indies have been careful to take with them seeds of every description. . . .

The trees that have fared best there are the orange, lemon, citron, and others of that sort. In some parts there are already whole forests and groves of orange trees. Marvelling at this, I asked on a certain island who had planted so many orange trees in the fields. To which they replied that it might have happened that some oranges fell to the ground and rotted, whereupon the seeds germinated, and, some being borne by the waters to different parts, gave rise to these dense groves. This seemed a likely reason. I said before that orange trees have generally done well in the Indies, for nowhere have I found a place where oranges were not to be found. . . .

Peaches and apricots also have done well, although the latter have fared better in New Spain. . . . Apples and pears are grown, but in moderate yields; plums give sparingly; figs are abundant, chiefly in Peru. Quinces are found everywhere, and in New Spain they are so plentiful that we received fifty choice ones for half a *real*. Pomegranates are found in abundance, but they are all sweet, for the people do not like the sharp variety. The melons are very good in some regions, as in Tierra Firme and Peru. Cherries, both wild and cultivated, have not so far prospered in the Indies. . . . In conclusion, I find that hardly any of the finer fruits is lacking in those parts. . . .

By profitable plants I mean those plants which not only yield fruit but bring money to their owners. The most important of these is the vine, which gives wine, vinegar, grapes, raisins, verjuice, and syrup—but the wine is the chief concern. Wine and grapes are not products of the islands or of Tierra Firme; in New Spain there are vines which bear grapes but do not yield wine. The reason must be that the grapes do not ripen completely because of the rains which come in July and August and hinder their ripening; they are good only for eating. Wine is shipped from Spain and the Canary Islands to all parts of the Indies, except Peru and Chile, where they have vineyards and make very good wine. This industry is expanding continually, not only because of the goodness of the soil, but because they have a better knowledge of winemaking. . . .

The silk which is made in New Spain goes to other provinces—to Peru, for example. There was no silk industry before the Spaniards came; the mulberry trees were brought from Spain, and they grow well, especially in the province called Misteca, where they raise silkworms and make good taffetas; they do not yet make damasks, satins, or velvets, however.

The sugar industry is even wider in scope, for the sugar not only is consumed in the Indies but is shipped in quantity to Spain. Sugar cane grows remarkably well in various parts of the Indies. In the islands, in Mexico, in Peru, and elsewhere they have built sugar mills that do a large business. I was told that the Nasca [Peru] sugar mill earned more than thirty thousand pesos a year. The mill at Chicama, near Trujillo [Peru], was also a big enterprise, and those of New Spain are no smaller, for the consumption of sugar and preserves in the Indies is simply fantastic. From the island of Santo Domingo, in the fleet in which I came, they brought eight hundred and ninety-eight chests and boxes of sugar. I happened to see the sugar loaded at the port of Puerto Rico, and it seemed to me that each box must contain eight *arrobas*.

The sugar industry is the principal business of those islands—such a taste have men developed for sweets!

Olives and olive trees are also found in the Indies, in Mexico, and in Peru, but up to now they have not set up any mills to make olive oil. Actually, it is not made at all, for they prefer to eat the olives, seasoning them well. They find it unprofitable to make olive oil, and so all their oil comes from Spain.

Questions

---

1. *How does Columbus portray the indigenous peoples? Does he present contradictory images of them? How does he gather his information about the customs, beliefs, and culture of the Amerindians when he does not speak their language? What role do you think Columbus envisioned for the indigenous peoples after the Europeans established their control?*

2. *Why did Las Casas and other clergymen present such an idealized picture of the Amerindians? Why did they picture the Spanish settlers as such barbarians? Do you think these portrayals are accurate or mere propaganda? Why?*

3. *What role did disease have in the European victories over the Amerindian empires of Mesoamerica and South America? Do the two indigenous accounts indicate that the Amerindians submitted passively to Spanish rule after the initial victories of the conquistadores? What factors do you think gave rise to the success of the Europeans?*

4. *Why did the people, plants, and animals of Europe fare so well in the New World? To what extent was the expansion of Europe made possible by this success? To what extent was the so-called Columbian exchange of plants, animals, and biota beneficial for the world?*

FURTHER READING

The literature on Christopher Columbus and his historical legacies is immense, but the standard treatment in English is by William D. Phillips, Jr. and Carla Rahn Phillips, The Worlds of Christopher Columbus *(New York, 1992). An older but still stimulating treatment of the impact of European expansion in the Caribbean is Carl Ortwin Sauer,* The Early Spanish Main *(Berkeley, 1966). An updated and expanded book on the ecological impact of global interdependency is by Alfred W. Crosby, Jr.,* Ecological Imperialism: The Biological Expansion of Europe, 900–1900 *(New York, 1986). A positive scholarly treatment of the life and times of Christopher Columbus is P. E. Taviani,* Christopher Columbus: The Grand Design *(London, 1985). A challenging literary treatment of the "encounters" in the New World is by Peter Hulme,* Colonial Encounters: Europe and the Native Caribbean, 1492–1797 *(New York, 1986).*

The Mayflower Compact

In 1606, King James of England laid claim to all the land along the eastern portion of North America from the thirty-fourth parallel to the forty-fifth parallel. The area in between the thirty-fourth and the thirty-eighth parallel was granted to the Virginia Company, a joint-stock venture. The so-called Plymouth group was granted control over the land between the forty-first and forty-fifth parallels, and the land in between was open to settlement by people from both groups. Unlike the settlers of the Chesapeake Bay region, the colonists of the Plymouth group came in search of peace and religious freedom rather than quick riches. Those aboard the Mayflower had been blown off course by a storm. Rather than landing near Chesapeake Bay, they disembarked on Cape Cod and established the colony of Plymouth.

Since the group lacked a royal charter giving them claim to the land, the leaders of the group of 101 settlers wrote the following Mayflower Compact establishing a government for their tiny community and claiming legitimate ownership of the land. It emphasized their relationship with God and their determination to found a godly community. Known also as "pilgrims," these settlers all followed a strict Protestant sect of Puritanism called Separatism. Even though their agreement acknowledges the political sovereignty of King James, their religious group had decisively split from the Church of England, Anglicanism, of which King James was the spiritual head. Anglicanism had been established by King Henry VIII in 1534 following a dispute with the Pope over the annulment of his marriage to Catherine of Aragon. The Puritan community had developed over the latter half of the sixteenth century with the aim of "purifying" the Church of England; essentially, Puritans believed that the Church of England was too Catholic and that it did not follow the path established by other strains of Protestantism, such as Lutheranism

---

From *Great Charters of Americanism* (Iowa City, 1920), 5.

and Calvinism, as closely as it should. Separatists, such as the pilgrims, had renounced the goal of reforming the Church of England, and sought instead to establish a separate, religiously-pure community.

In the name of God, Amen. We, whose names are underwritten, the loyal subjects of our dread sovereign Lord, King James, by the grace of God, of Great Britain, France and Ireland king, defender of the faith, etc., having undertaken for the glory of God, and advancement of the Christian faith, and honor of our king and country, a voyage to plant the first colony in the northern parts of Virginia, do, by these presents solemnly and mutually in the presence of God, and one of another, covenant and combine ourselves together into a civil body politic, for our better ordering and preservation and furtherance of the ends aforesaid; and by virtue hereof to enact, constitute, and frame such just and equal laws, ordinances, acts, constitutions, and offices, from time to time, as shall be thought most meet and convenient for the general good of the colony, unto which we promise all due submission and obedience. In witness whereof we have hereunder subscribed our names at Cape Cod the 11th of November, in the year of the reign of our sovereign Lord, King James, of England, France and Ireland, the eighteenth, and of Scotland, the fifty-fourth. Anno. Dom. 1620.

The Salem
Witchcraft Scare

Carla Gardina Pestana

INTRODUCTION

English colonists brought with them beliefs about witches and, once in America, occasionally suspected some residents of practicing witchcraft. According to contemporary wisdom, witches entered into a pact with Satan and thereby acquired supernatural powers. They used these powers to harm their neighbors, in acts of witchcraft known as maleficum. Individuals were suspected of witchcraft in many English colonies in the seventeenth century, including Connecticut, Maryland, Massachusetts, the Somers Island (or Bermuda), and Virginia. Nowhere in Anglo-America, however, were more witches accused than in Massachusetts, the most populous and powerful of the "Puritan" colonies of New England. The bulk of the accusations and trials there occurred in 1692 in the northeastern part of the colony, in a witchcraft scare that has come to be associated with the town of Salem, where the outbreak began.

In 1692, some residents of the coastal town of Salem became convinced that many of their neighbors had become witches. The scare began with a group of adolescent girls and young women who were dabbling in occult practices in an effort to learn about the future. When a number of them fell into strange fits, a physician diagnosed these as the work of a witch. The afflicted then made a series of accusations, adult community members supported their charges and fingered others, and the "witch hunt" was on.

At the time of the outbreak the colony had only a provisional government, while it awaited a new royal charter and the arrival of a governor. (This state of uncertainty had developed since the revocation of the charter in 1686. At that time, the colony had been subsumed under a new "Dominion of New England," but it later rose in revolt hoping to get support from King William and Queen Mary for a return to its old charter. This support had not materialized, so the colony rather nervously awaited a new charter and a new governor in 1692.) With no legitimate claim to govern, the colony's leaders were loath to try capital crimes such as witchcraft. So, as the number of accused witches soared to over a hundred, the authorities simply jailed the suspects while awaiting word from England. By the time the new governor, Sir William Phipps, arrived, the jails were overflowing. Many colonists were certain that witches were conspiring to take over the colony. The governor appointed an emergency court with broad powers to try the cases and it ordered nineteen people hanged in the months that followed.

The crisis came to a close that autumn for a number of reasons. Popular support for the trials waned as more individuals with good reputations (some of them drawn from the ranks of the elites) were accused. The populace may also have felt revulsion at the violence of the many executions. When a group of ministers led by the influential Increase Mather publicly questioned some of the evidence the judges were accepting, the authority of the court was seriously undermined. In October the governor replaced the first court with a new one that had more limited powers; his instructions to the second court indicated a need for greater restraint. He reprieved the few witches that it did convict and then granted a general pardon, emptying the jails of the remaining suspects.

Participants in the trials and scholars subsequently have struggled to make sense of one of the most dramatic and disturbing episodes in colonial history. After 1692, colonists gave up the practice of witch hunting, and no major outbreak followed the one that has made Salem infamous. But colonists were slower to give up their belief that the devil played an active role in their lives. Indeed, the first attempts to explain what had gone wrong at Salem attributed the debacle to a "delusion of Satan" that caused the community to see a witch conspiracy where none existed. Since that time, many interpretations have been offered to explain the witchcraft crisis. Modern Americans, inclined to believe that the religious bigotry of the Puritans can explain anything distressing in their history, find it surprising that the ministers helped to halt the trials. Other aspects of the witch scare may surprise you as well.

WHO WAS ACCUSED OF WITCHCRAFT AND WHY: SCHOLARS' EXPLANATIONS

The selections below, taken from recent histories of the witchcraft scare, all grapple with the question: What motivated the accusations? All four historians identify specific groups in the society liable to be the objects of witchcraft charges. And they all suggest that late-seventeenth-century Massachusetts was gripped by social tensions of one sort or another, tensions that led to the fears that sparked the charges against members of these suspect groups.

Whichever argument you find most appealing, it is important to recall that everyone in seventeenth-century New England believed in the existence of witches with the power to do harm. What is at issue here is whom among their neighbors did they identify as members of that frightening group.

Economic and Political Causes

The first excerpt outlines economic and political divisions in the community. Abridged from Paul Boyer and Stephen Nissenbaum, "Salem Possessed: The Social Origins of Witchcraft," in Colonial America: Essays in Politics and Social Development, *ed. Stanley N. Katz and John M. Murrin, 3d ed. (New York, 1983), 346–53, 358–59, 361, 363–65.*

The first three women to be accused can be seen as "deviants" or "outcasts" in their community—the kinds of people who anthropologists have suggested are particularly susceptible to such accusations. Tituba was a West Indian slave; Sarah Good was a pauper who went around the Village begging aggressively for food and lodging; "Gammer" Osborne, while somewhat better off, was a bedridden old woman.

In March, however, a new pattern began to emerge. Two of the three witches accused in that month—the third was little Dorcas Good—were church members (a sign of real respectability in the seventeenth century) and the wives of prosperous freeholders. This pattern continued and even intensified for the duration of the outbreak. The twenty-two persons accused in April included the wealthiest shipowner in Salem (Phillip English) and a minister of the gospel who was a Harvard graduate with a considerable estate in England (George Burroughs). By mid-May warrants had been issued against two of the seven selectmen of Salem Town; and by the end of the summer some of the most prominent people in Massachusetts and their close kin had been accused if not officially charged. As the attorney who prepared the cases against the accused wrote at the end of May, "The afflicted spare no person of what quality so ever."

True, except for Burroughs, none of these persons of quality was ever brought to trial, much less executed. Some escaped from jail or house arrest, others were simply never arraigned. Nevertheless, the overall direction of the accusations remains clear: up the social ladder, fitfully but perceptibly, to its very top. Whatever else they may have been, the Salem witch trials cannot be written off as a communal effort to purge the poor, the deviant, or the outcast.

Just as the accusations thrust steadily upward through the social strata of provincial society, so, too, they pressed outward across geographic boundaries. Beginning within Salem Village itself, the accusations moved steadily into an increasingly wide orbit. The first twelve witches were either residents of the Village or persons who lived just beyond its borders. But of all the indictments which followed this initial dozen, only fifteen were directed against people in the immediate vicinity of Salem Village. The other victims came from virtually every town in Essex

County, including the five which surrounded the Village. (In the town of Andover alone, there were more arrests than in Salem Village itself.)

While almost all these arrests were made on the basis of testimony given by the ten or so afflicted girls of Salem Village (although in some cases they merely confirmed the validity of others' accusations), it is clear that the girls themselves did not actually know most of the people they named. Accusers and accused were in many if not most cases personally unacquainted. Whatever was troubling the girls and those who encouraged them, it was something deeper than the kind of chronic, petty squabbles between near neighbors which seem to have been at the root of earlier and far less severe witchcraft episodes in New England.

But if the outbreak's geographic pattern tends to belie certain traditional explanations, it raises other, more intriguing, interpretive possibilities. As Map 1 shows, there were fourteen accused witches who lived within the bounds of Salem Village. Twelve of these fourteen lived in the eastern section of the Village.

There were thirty-two adult Villagers who testified against these accused witches. Only two of these lived in that eastern section. The other thirty lived on the western side. In other words, the alleged witches and those who accused them resided on opposite sides of the Village.

There were twenty-nine villagers who publicly showed their skepticism about the trials or came to the defense of one or more of the accused witches. Twenty-four of these lived in the eastern part of the Village—the same side on which the witches lived—and only two of them in the west. Those who defended the witches were generally their neighbors, often their immediate neighbors. Those who accused them were not.

. . . Even before 1692 Salem Village had hardly been a haven of tranquility. For years its 600-odd residents had been divided into two bitterly antagonistic factions. The source of their troubles lay in the very circumstances under which the Village had first come into existence. Originally the settlement (which is now the city of Danvers, and not to be confused with Salem proper) had simply been a part of the town of Salem, and when it was granted a limited and partial legal existence as "Salem Village" in 1672, it still remained in many ways a mere appendage of its larger and more prosperous neighbor. Some people in the Village were quite

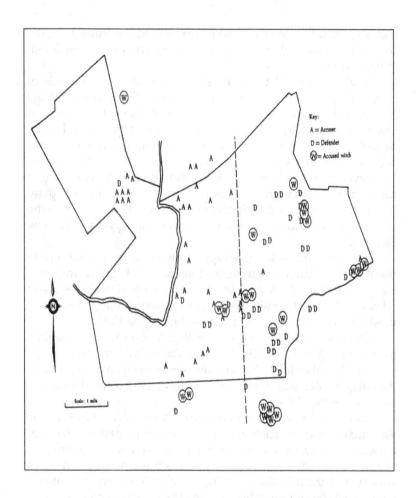

Map 1 The Geography of Witchcraft: Salem Village, 1692

Sources: Residential map of Salem Village in 1692 included as a frontispiece to volume one of Charles W. Upham, *Salem Witchcraft*, 22 vols. (Boston, 1867); W. Elliot Woodward, *Records of Salem Witchcraft Copied from the Original Documents*, 2 vols. (Roxbury, Mass., Privately printed, 1864; reissued in one volume, New York, Da Capo Press, 1969).

content with this satellite status, but others resented it and pressed for complete independence. The latter group, led by a numerous and powerful local family named Putnam, focused its efforts on an attempt to establish a separate church—the central pillar of any Puritan town. . . .

At last in 1689, however, the independence-minded group in Salem Village managed to get its way, and a church was formed under the ministry of Samuel Parris, a thirty-six-year-old former merchant. But this victory was purchased at a heavy price, for the new minister, and the church he headed, represented only a single group in the community—a group led by the Putnams. (Fully half of the original twenty-six church members bore the Putnam name!) The formation of the church, in short, did not serve to unify Salem Village, but only to intensify its inner divisions.

. . . Those Villagers who had all along opposed establishment of the church, and who now refused to join it—a group that included some of the community's wealthiest residents—determined to drive Parris out of his position. They refused to worship in the Village meetinghouse, pointedly attending elsewhere, and withheld payment of their local taxes (which went for the minister's salary and firewood). But their most deadly stroke came at the annual Village election in October 1691 when they swept out of office the existing five-man Village Committee (the local equivalent of a board of selectmen), dominated by Parris' friends, and elected a new Committee made up, to a man, of his known opponents.

The new anti-Parris Committee went quickly to work: it refused even to assess taxes for the payment of Parris' 1692 salary, and it challenged the legality of his "fraudulent" acquisition of the ministry-house and lands in 1689. Parris, now wholly dependent on the voluntary contributions of his supporters for money to purchase the necessities of life—and even for firewood to heat his house—was in desperately serious trouble at the beginning of 1692, and his Putnam supporters knew it.

Thus we begin to see the significance of the fact that of the first four "afflicted girls" in Salem Village, two lived in the household of Samuel Parris himself, and a third, Ann Putnam, was the twelve-year-old daughter of Parris' most dogged supporter, Thomas Putnam Jr. (In the coming weeks, the Thomas Putnam household would produce two more afflicted girls: Mercy Lewis, a servant girl, and Mary Walcott, a young relative.)

Samuel Parris (1653–1720) served as minister in Salem Village in 1692. The Witchcraft scare began in his home, with various women of his household, including his slave Tituba, involved. Historians have placed some of the blame for the unprecedented number of executions at his door. (Courtesy of Massachusetts Historical Society.)

While these girls themselves may well have been unacquainted with the details of factional politics in the Village, they could hardly have remained untouched by the bitterness and resentment that pervaded their own households. It may be no accident that their physical torments set in after they had attempted, with scary results, to predict the future—a future that loomed as highly uncertain not only for the girls themselves but for the adults they knew best. . . .

. . . [T]he richest men in the Village opposed Parris by a margin of better than two-to-one, while the poorest supported him in almost precisely the same proportion. . . . [Those] who lived nearest Salem Town (or, in a few cases, just over the Village line in the Town) opposed Parris by a ratio of six-to-one. Those whose houses were in the northwestern half of the Village, most remote from the Town, *supported* Parris by a ratio of better than four to one. . . . [N]ot every Villager had reason to feel alienated from the Town. Indeed, the economic and social transformation of the Town in these years affected different Villagers in quite different ways. The very developments which threatened many of them gave others reason to take heart. It was this fact, above all, that produced the factional lines which from the beginning divided the Village.

From the 1670's on, proximity to the Town, and even a direct involvement in its economic life, repeatedly emerged as a determining factor in the divisions which plagued the Village. These divisions pitted people who continued to identify with Salem

Town against others for whom the Village, and what they saw as its distinctive interests, were paramount. . . .

. . . In at least two important respects—quality of land and access to market—those farmers on the eastern (or Town) side of the Village had a significant advantage. Modern topographical maps show what any Salem Village farmer knew from first-hand experience: the best lands in the Village were the broad, flat meadows of the eastern part, nearest the coast, while the western part was increasingly broken up by sharp little hills and marshy depressions. The eastern side of the Village, too, was significantly closer to the network of roads and waterways which gave access to Salem Town and her markets. (The additional two or three miles may seem negligible today, but for the farmer who had to convey his goods by ox cart over rutted, muddy, and often flooded paths before reaching the better-maintained Ipswich Road, they certainly loomed large.) In both these respects, then, the farmers on this side of the Village had a crucial edge in supplying the needs of Salem Town. . . .

More than any other inhabitants of the community, the Villagers who lived along the Ipswich Road were exposed to the Town and its concerns. . . . It is not surprising that a number of the men living on or very near the Ipswich Road were engaged in occupations which brought them into regular contact with a wide range of individuals: occupations such as potter, physician, carpenter, innkeeper, sawmill operator, shoemaker, miller, sawyer (that is, wood finisher), and "dishturner." Particularly important, in terms of the Townward orientation of this part of Salem Village, were the four taverns which stood along a short stretch of the Ipswich Road as it passed through Salem Village. Three of these actually lay within the Village: the licensed taverns of Joshua Rea, Jr. and Walter Phillips, and the unlicensed—but well known and well patronized—tavern of Edward and Bridget Bishop. The other, operated by John Proctor, stood about a mile south of the Village boundary. . . .

The pro-Parris faction thus emerges as a coalition whose shared fears united it in support of Parris: a core group of Villagers of middling wealth who were also church members, supplemented by another group, approximately twice as large, of poorer Villagers who were not church members but who identified with the Village church and its minister. The church members provided the institutional structure and the political impetus, the others supplied the votes and the signatures.

Since the pro-Parris faction also played a leading role in the witchcraft prosecutions, it has typically been portrayed as a powerful and domineering clique. From the evidence, however, this group emerges as by far the more vulnerable of the two: less wealthy than its opposition, owning less land, quite literally hedged in by more flourishing anti-Parris neighbors and less able to benefit from the commercial developments centered in Salem Town.

If the Ipswich Road helped shape and define the anti-Parris faction, it also provided an objective focus for the amorphous fears of the pro-Parris group, for whom it would have seemed not so much the line which separated the Village from the Town, but the very channel through which the Town penetrated the Village. The road stood as a perpetual affront to those who felt the integrity of the Village to be menaced from just this quarter. Its residents, with their more commercial outlook and occupations, had in many cases already succumbed to the lure which menaced the Village as a whole. . . .

A revealing glimpse into the social circumstances surrounding the establishment of one of these taverns emerges from John Proctor's request to the Salem selectmen in 1666 for a license to operate a tavern in his house on the Ipswich Road near the Salem Village line. His residence, he said, was "in the common roadway, which occasioneth several travelers to call in for some refreshment as they pass along." Since the free entertaining of these wayfarers was proving to be expensive, Proctor added: "I do therefore earnestly request that you would be pleased to grant me liberty to set up a house of entertainment to sell beer, cider [and] liquors." The court granted Proctor's petition, with the stipulation that he sell exclusively to strangers. Thus, from the Salem Village perspective, the Proctor house became a rendezvous point for outsiders—and *only* for outsiders.

For the pro-Parris Salem Villagers, with their particular anxieties, this generalized concern over taverns must have been especially intense. Given such a background, it is not surprising to find that three of the four Ipswich Road tavern keepers figured prominently in the climatic Village events of the 1690's—and two of these three as victims of those events. Joshua Rea, Jr., publicly expressed his opposition to the witchcraft trials in 1692 by signing a petition seeking to save Rebecca Nurse from the gallows. In 1695 Rea's name appears on the anti-Parris petition. Two of the other tavern keepers, Bridget Bishop and John Proctor, were unable to take a stand for or against Parris in 1695: they had been hanged three years before for committing witchcraft.

Gender Tensions

The following selection examines the gender issues at play in the witch-craft scare at Salem and in other accusations made in colonial New England. Taken fron Carol Karlsen, The Devil in the Shape of a Woman: Witchcraft in Colonial New England *(New York, 1987), 47–48, 50–52, 101–2, 104, 107–8, 115–16.*

The single most salient characteristic of witches was their sex. At least 344 persons were accused of witchcraft in New England between 1620 and 1725. Of the 342 who can be identified by sex, 267 (78 percent) were female. Roughly half of the seventy-five males accused (thirty-six), as the historian John Demos has pointed out, were "suspect by association": they were the husbands, sons, other kin, or public supporters of female witches. . . .

The idea that witches were women seems to have been more strongly held by local authorities, magistrates, and juries—men who had the power to decide the fates of the accused—than it was by accusers as a whole. This bias is most noticeable in non-outbreak witchcraft cases: although women made up a sizeable 83 percent of the accused in these cases, and although local officials sent roughly the same proportion of female and male suspects to the colony-wide courts for trial, fifteen of the sixteen *convicted* witches (94 percent) were women. . . . The only man to be found guilty was Wethersfield carpenter John Carrington, who was hanged with his wife Joan in 1651. Though he was married to a reputed witch and was one of the poorest men in his community, it remains unclear why, leaving outbreaks aside, he was the only man to receive a punishment normally reserved for women. . . .

Statistics can establish the extent to which New Englanders considered witchcraft the special province of women, but they

Sex of Witches, Salem, 1692

	Female	Male	Total
Accused	141	44	185
Tried	52	7	59
Convicted	26	5	31
Executed	14	5	19

Adapted from a table in Karlsen, *The Devil in the Shape of a Woman.*

cannot convey the vindictiveness that characterized the treatment of female suspects. This sexual double standard is perhaps most vividly seen in the different punishments meted out to confessed witches outside of the Salem outbreak.

Deeming voluntary confession one of the best "proofes sufficient for Conviccion," ministers and magistrates put considerable pressure on women to admit they had covenanted with the Devil. No comparable coercion was used with men. When Wethersfield's Mary Johnson succumbed to this insistence in 1648, admitting that she and the Devil provided many services for one another, she was convicted of familiarity with Satan and hanged. After Rebecca Greensmith described the nature of her covenant with Satan in Hartford in 1662, she too was executed. Similarly, confession doomed the widow Glover in Boston in 1688. Except during the Salem events, when the magistrates decided to put off the executions of people who admitted their guilt until all local witches were discovered, women who incriminated themselves were almost all punished in accordance with the biblical injunction, "Thou shall not suffer a witch to live."

Men who incriminated themselves were treated quite differently. When John Bradstreet of Rowley confessed in 1652 to having familiarity with Satan, the Essex County court ordered him whipped or fined "for telling a lie." In 1674, Christopher Brown was also released by Essex County magistrates, on the grounds that *his* confession seemed "inconsistent with the truth," despite his admission that he had been "discoursing with . . . the devil." Though Hugh Crosia of Stratford confessed in 1692 that he had "signed to the devells book and then seald it with his bloud" five years earlier, and that ever since he had "been practising Eivel against Every man," the Connecticut Court of Assistants refused to try him, discharging him upon payment of his jail fees and the costs of bringing him to Hartford. Men who confessed to witch-craft outside of the Salem outbreak were punished, to be sure—but whereas most confessing women were taken at their word and executed, confessing men were almost all rebuked as liars. Even when the courts took charges against individual men more seriously, their responses to these men were noticeably less severe than were their responses to the women whose cases they acted upon. As the following accounts illustrate, the repercussions of an accusation were likely to be far graver and longer lasting for a woman than for a man, even when their personal circumstances and the evidence were strikingly similar. . . .

[Karlsen then provides a detailed account of six women's experiences.]

. . . The six women featured in these histories were either (1) daughters of parents who had no sons (or whose sons had died), (2) women in marriages which brought forth only daughters (or in which the sons had died), or (3) women in marriages with no children at all. These patterns had significant economic implications. Because there were no legitimate male heirs in their immediate families, each of these six women stood to inherit, did inherit, or were denied their apparent right to inherit substantially larger portions of their fathers' or husbands' accumulated estates than women in families with male heirs. Whatever actually happened to the property in question—and in some cases we simply do not know—these women were aberrations in a society with an inheritance system designed to keep property in the hands of men.

These six cases also illustrate fertility and mortality patterns widely shared among the families of accused witches. A substantial majority of New England's accused females were women without brothers, women with daughters but no sons, or women in marriages with no children at all. . . . Of the 267 accused females, enough is known about 158 to identify them as either having or not having brothers or sons to inherit: only sixty-two of the 158 (39 percent) did, whereas ninety-six (61 percent) did not. More striking, *once accused*, women without brothers or sons were even more likely than women with brothers or sons to be tried, convicted, and executed: women from families without male heirs made up 64 percent of the females prosecuted, 76 percent of those who were found guilty, and 89 percent of those who were executed. . . .

Numbers alone, however, do not tell the whole story. More remains to be said about what happened to these inheriting or potentially inheriting women, both before and after they were accused of witchcraft.

It was not unusual for women in families without male heirs to be accused of witchcraft shortly after the deaths of fathers, husbands, brothers, or sons. . . . Not all witches from families without male heirs were accused of conspiring with the Devil *after* they had come into their inheritances. On the contrary, some were accused prior to the death of the crucial male relative, many times before it was clear who would inherit. Eunice Cole was one of these women. Another was Martha Corey of Salem, who was accused of witchcraft in 1692 while her husband was still alive. Giles Corey had been married twice before and had several daughters by the time he married the widow Martha Rich, probably in the 1680s. With no sons to inherit, Giles's substantial land holdings would, his neighbors might have assumed, be passed on to his wife and daughters. Alice Parker, who may have been Giles's daughter from a former marriage, also came before the magistrates as a witch in 1692, as did Giles himself. Martha Corey and Alice Parker maintained their innocence and were hanged. Giles Corey, in an apparently futile attempt to preserve his whole estate for his heirs, refused to respond to the indictment. To force him to enter a plea, he was tortured: successively heavier weights were placed on his body until he was pressed to death.

What seems especially significant here is that most accused witches whose husbands were still alive were, like their counterparts who were widows and spinsters, over forty years of age—and therefore unlikely if not unable to produce male heirs. Indeed, the fact that witchcraft accusations were rarely taken seriously by the community until the accused stopped bearing children takes on a special meaning when it is juxtaposed with the anomolous position of inheriting women or potentially inheriting women in New England's social structure.

Witches in families without male heirs sometimes had been dispossessed of part or all of their inheritances before—sometimes long before—they were formally charged with witchcraft. Few of these women, however, accepted disinheritance with equanimity. Rather, like Susanna Martin, they took their battles to court, casting themselves in the role of public challengers to the system of male inheritance. In most instances, the authorities sided with their antagonists. . . .

Looking back over the lives of these many women—most particularly those who did not have brothers or sons to inherit—we begin to understand the complexity of the economic dimension of New England witchcraft. Only rarely does the actual trial testimony indicate that economic power was even at issue. Nevertheless it is there, recurring with a telling persistence once we look beyond what was explicitly said about these women as witches. Inheritance disputes surface frequently enough in witchcraft cases, cropping up as part of the general context even when no direct link between the dispute and the charge is discernible, to suggest the fears that underlay most accusations. No matter how deeply entrenched the principle of male inheritance, no matter how carefully written the laws that protected it, it was impossible to insure that all families had male offspring. The women who stood to benefit from these demographic "accidents" account for most of New England's female witches. . . .

. . . If daughters, husbands, and sons of witches were more vulnerable to danger in 1692 than they had been previously, they were mostly the daughters, husbands, and sons of inheriting or potentially inheriting women. As the outbreak spread, it drew into its orbit increasing numbers of women, "unlikely" witches in that they were married to well-off and influential men, but familiar figures to some of their neighbors nonetheless. What the impoverished Sarah Good had in common with Mary Phips, wife of Massachusetts's governor, was what Eunice Cole had in common with Katherine Harrison, and what Mehitabel Downing had in common with Ann Hibbens. However varied their backgrounds and economic positions, as women without brothers or women without sons, they stood in the way of the orderly transmission of property from one generation of males to another.

Character Traits

John Demos, after suggesting that the witch prosecutions cannot be described as simply a war of the sexes, offers an explanation that relies largely on individual personality traits. Like Karlsen, Demos looks at evidence from other witchcraft cases rather than just from Salem. Abridged from John Putnam Demos, Entertaining Satan: Witchcraft and the Culture of Early New England *(New York, 1982), 63–64, 86, 89, 91–94.*

An easy hypothesis—perhaps too easy—would make of witchcraft a single plank in a platform of "sexist" oppression. Presumably, the threat of being charged as a witch might serve to constrain the behavior of women. Those who asserted themselves too openly or forcibly could expect a summons to court, and risked incurring the ultimate sanction of death itself. Hence the dominance of *men* would be underscored in both symbolic and practical terms. Male dominance was, of course, an assumed principle in traditional society—including the society of early New England. Men controlled political life; they alone could vote and hold public office. Men were also leaders in religion, as pastors and elders of local congregations. Men owned the bulk of personal property (though women had some rights and protections). Furthermore, the values of the culture affirmed the "headship" of men in marital and family relations and their greater "wisdom" in everyday affairs. Certainly, then, the uneven distribution of witchcraft accusations and their special bearing on the lives of women were consistent with sex-roles generally.

But was there *more* to this than simple consistency? Did the larger matrix of social relations enclose some dynamic principle that would energize actual "witch-hunting" so as to hold women down? On this the evidence—at least from early New England—seems doubtful. There is little sign of generalized (or "structural") conflict between the sexes. Male dominance of public affairs was scarcely an issue, and in private life there was considerable scope for female initiative. Considered overall, the relations of men and women were less constrained by differences of role and status than would be the case for most later generations of Americans. It is true that many of the suspects displayed qualities of assertiveness and aggressiveness beyond what the culture deemed proper. But these displays were not directed at men as such; often enough the targets were other women. Moreover, no single line in the extant materials raises the issue of sex-defined patterns of authority. Thus, if witches were at some level protesters against male oppression, they themselves seem to have been

T.H. Matteson's 1855 painting Examination of a Witch *dramatized an imagined scene from the witch trials. By the middle of the nineteenth century, New Englanders were intrigued by the trials, and painters depicted the events based on a fairly crude understanding of what occured. In reality, a suspected witch's body would be examined for telltale signs by a delegation of women that would then report to the court. (Courtesy of Peabody Essex Museum.)*

unconscious of the fact. As much could be said of the accusers, in the (putative) impulse to dominate. . . .

And one final point in this connection: a large portion of witchcraft charges were brought against women *by* other women. Thus, if the fear of witchcraft expressed a deep strain of misogyny, it was something in which both sexes shared. . . .

With the witches' sex, age, personal background, family life, propensity to crime, occupations, and social position all accounted for (as best we can manage), there yet remains one category which may be the most important of all. What were these people like—as people? What range of motive, of style, and of behavior would they typically exhibit? Can the scattered artifacts of their separate careers be made to yield a composite portrait, a model, so to speak, of witch-character? . . .

. . . Witchcraft was *defined* in reference to conflict; and most charges of witchcraft grew out of specific episodes of conflict.

Hence it should not be surprising that the suspects, as individuals, were notably active that way. . . .

To be sure, most of the evidence on the motives and behavior of witches comes by way of their accusers; what, then, of its relation to "objective" reality? Perhaps such evidence should be viewed as inherently prejudiced, indeed as a reflection of the accusers' *own* character and inner preoccupations. This difficulty can be countered, if not entirely resolved, in several ways. For one thing, at least some of the pertinent testimony derives from situations which had nothing to do with witchcraft. . . . There are also various comments made in court *by* the suspects—in short, self-reports—to much the same effect. (Mary Johnson declared that general "discontent" had tempted her to invoke the Devil. Katherine Harrison apologized for slandering her neighbors with "hasty, unadvised, and passionate expressions." Hugh Parsons admitted that "in his anger he is impatient, and doth speak what he should not.") Finally, there is the simple probability that so much opinion, of such a broadly convergent sort, cannot entirely misrepresent actual experience—the proverbial "fire" burning unseen but rightly inferred behind a cloud of all-too-evident "smoke." Hostile characterization usually finds some truth on which to fasten, even where it also expresses a deeply subjective concern. . . .

However disagreeable they seemed to their peers, the suspects were tough, resilient, purposive. John Godfrey was not merely a frequent litigant; he was also a determined and successful one. Anne Hibbens would bend, but never break, in the face of unanimous censure by her brethren in the Boston church. Katherine Harrison countered the animus of her Wethersfield neighbors by way of formal actions at court and informal (personally given) rebuke. Indeed it was this configuration of qualities that made the individuals involved seem not only suspect but genuinely fearsome. Had they been "crazed," "distracted," or "impotent . . . in understanding," their words and deeds would not have counted for very much. In reality, they seemed anything

---

"Specters of Subversion, Societies of Friends: Dissent and the Devil in Provincial Essex County, Massachusetts," by Christine Leigh Heyrman, reprinted from *Saints and Revolutionaries—Essays on Early American History*, David D. Hall, John M. Murrin, and Thad W. Tate, editors. Reprinted with permission of W. W. Norton & Company, Inc. Copyright © 1984 by W. W. Norton & Company, Inc.

but "impotent." Their general ill will, their presumed envies and resentments, their explicit threats to do harm would all be treated with the utmost seriousness precisely because, in a certain sense, they were *strong.* . . .

From this long and somewhat tortuous exercise in prosopography a rough composite finally emerges. To recapitulate, the typical witch:

1. was female.
2. was of middle age (i.e. between forty and sixty years old).
3. was of English (and "Puritan") background.
4. was married, but was more likely (than the general population) to have few children—or none at all.
5. was frequently involved in trouble and conflict with other family members.
6. had been accused, on some previous occasion, of committing crimes—most especially theft, slander, or other forms of assaultive speech.
7. was more likely (than the general population) to have professed and practiced a medical vocation, i.e. "doctoring" on a local, quite informal basis.
8. was of relatively low social position.
9. was abrasive in style, contentious in character—and stubbornly resilient in the face of adversity.

Religious Tensions

Finally, Christine Heyrman puts forth the only thesis considered here that places religion at the center of the controversy: she asserts that associates of the small community of Quaker dissenters were especially likely to be targeted. Excerpted from Christine Heyrman, "Specters of Subversion, Societies of Friends: Dissent and the Devil in Provincial Essex County, Massachusetts," in Saints and Revolutionaries: Essays on Early American History, *ed. David D. Hall, John M. Murrin, and Thad W. Tate (New York, 1984), 47–48, 51–53, 55.*

Even before her alleged bewitchment in the fall of 1692, Mary Stevens had probably become an object of local concern because of her courtship by Francis Norwood, Jr., the Quaker grandson of Clement Coldom. The marriage of Mary to Francis would not have been the first merging of orthodox and dissenting families in Gloucester, but it was a union of tremendous social significance. For Mary was not a servant maid or the daughter of an ordinary local farmer up in Goose Cove, but the child of Deacon James Stevens of the First Church, one of Gloucester's most prominent citizens; and Francis was not the stepson of an obscure Quaker farmer, but an avowed Friend from a fairly affluent family. Francis's suit of Mary Stevens thus marked the first movement of the Friends in Gloucester out of their position on the periphery of local society and the neighborhood of the remote northern Cape and into the mainstream. Their betrothal persuaded Lt. William Stevens, Mary's older brother and a major local merchant, that only demonic influences could have prevailed upon his sister to accept the attentions of a Quaker. As alarmed by the discovery of dissenting affinities among his own kin as Clement Coldom had been earlier, William Stevens acted to defend his family's integrity and to dissuade his sister from a disastrous alliance by declaring that she was bewitched. Stevens also sent for four of Salem Village's "afflicted girls," the instigators of the witchcraft trials held earlier in 1692, who claimed to have the power to discern who troubled the victims of malefic magic. But when William Stevens sought assistance from Salem Village, he and his neighbors already suspected who had bewitched his sister—her prospective father-in-law, Francis Norwood, Sr., whom everyone in Gloucester had long believed to be a wizard. . . .

What endows the story of Mary Stevens with some importance for understanding the history of heterodoxy in Massachusetts is that this case was not singular. In fact, the same fears of heresy's infecting orthodox families through intermarriage or other ties to dissenters that stirred William Stevens underlay many of the other witchcraft prosecutions in Essex County during 1692. The center of the hysteria that had peaked earlier in that year was Salem, the town with the largest concentration of Quakers in the county. As in Gloucester, the connection in Salem between actual prosecutions for witchcraft and religious heterodoxy was indirect: few Quakers, and none of Essex County's most prominent Friends, were accused of the crime. The situation in Salem differed from the Stevens possession in Gloucester in only one way: here it was the "witches" rather than the bewitched who had ties of blood, marriage, affection, or friendship to the Quakers. But many of the Salem trials, like the Stevens case, reflect the same anxieties over the merging of the orthodox and dissenting communities. A substantial number of the witches accused by Salem Village's "afflicted girls" came from families or households that included Quaker members. A case in point is the apparently puzzling prosecution of Rebecca Nurse. The pattern of indictments in Salem conformed to that of Andover and Gloucester insofar as those initially accused were all social outcasts in some sense—poor or shrewish women prone to violent or unseemly behavior, and usually reputed to have practiced malefic magic against their neighbors. The sole exception was Rebecca Nurse, a paragon of matronly piety, a pillar of respectability, a church member, and the wife of a substantial Salem Village farmer, Francis. There was only one reason that her neighbors had for disliking Rebecca Nurse: namely, that in 1677 the young Samuel Southwick, the orphaned son of a local Quaker farmer, John Southwick, chose the Nurses as his guardians and that they took the boy into their home. Rebecca and Francis were not Quakers, but their ward was.

Among those accused of witchcraft later in the trial proceedings were a large number of people who shared with Rebecca Nurse the same kind of indirect Quaker affinities, connections of kinship, and friendship with religious dissidents. There was the Proctor family, for example, of which five members—John, his wife, Elizabeth, and three of their children—were charged with witchcraft. What made the Proctors suspect in the eyes of their neighbors was less that John ran a tavern on the Ipswich Road than that his wife's family, the Bassets of Lynn, included a large number of Quakers. . . .

Along with the bonds of blood and marriage, geographic propinquity to the Quaker community characterized many of the accused witches of Salem Village. Since most of these accused witches lived in Salem Village's more prosperous eastern part, situated adjacent to Salem Town, and since the majority of the accusers came from the more remote and economically stagnant western side, it has been suggested that western farmers both envied and resented the east's exposure to the affluent, cosmopolitan town. But more prominent in the thinking of the western Villagers than the greater proximity of their eastern neighbors to commercial Salem Town may have been the even shorter physical distance separating the residences of the accused from Salem's Quaker enclave. . . .

. . . [T]ypically the accused witches were not themselves members of dissenting sects, and their connections with heterodoxy consisted in more tangential ties to dissenters among blood relatives, in-laws, household members, or neighbors and friends. Even in the case of Abigail Somes, accusations passed over Samuel Gaskill, for decades a central figure in the Salem Meeting, and focused instead on his ward, the child of an orthodox father and a heretical mother. Her background and that of many other accused witches suggest that the focus of anxiety was less on dissenters themselves than on those individuals who because of their relations or residences fell under suspicion of harboring if not heterodox sympathies then at least sympathy for the heterodox. The very ambiguity of their affinities and the division of their religious loyalties by the ties of family and friendship made such figures even more threatening to the maintenance of orthodoxy than known dissenters.

Questions

---

1. *What explanation offered by these scholars do you find the most convincing?*
2. *Demos, writing prior to Karlsen, criticizes a simplistic explanation that relies on sex roles; do you believe that Karlsen has answered his objections in her analysis of the role of gender?*
3. *The excerpts by Boyer and Nissenbaum and Heyrman both refer to residential patterns in the accusations; whose interpretation do you find most convincing?*
4. *Can you think of any way to tie these various theories about who would be accused together: Is there, for instance, an underlying theme to unite them all?*

CONTEMPORARY IDEAS ABOUT WITCHES AND THE EVENTS AT SALEM

The documents that follow examine Salem witchcraft from a number of different perspectives. The case against Bridget Bishop includes depositions taken largely from lay people who came forward to accuse this woman of witchcraft. The statement by a group of ministers lays out the somewhat belated clerical opposition to the trials, which played a key role in ending them. The documents authored by Increase and Cotton Mather present some of their views, penned either while the trials were still going on or ten years after they had ended. Together, these documents provide a glimpse of attitudes toward the supernatural in late-seventeenth-century New England.

The Case Against Bridget Bishop

One of nineteen people executed as a witch in 1692, Bridget Bishop had some of the classic attributes her New England neighbors were inclined to associate with a witch. For one thing, she was alienated from the religious faith of the community, having never attended worship services. In addition, she ran a tavern, where excessive drinking and game playing were common. She seems to have been seen as embodying relaxed sexual attitudes; deponents elsewhere mention her red bodice and a number of men may have had illicit thoughts about her, as they recount nocturnal visits to their beds by her specter (or ethereal image).

The excerpts below from the depositions taken against her offer typical examples of behavior attributed to alleged witches: she caused illness or death to people and animals, her image could appear as a specter, and she could change herself into other shapes. On one count, however, Bridget Bishop was unique. Only she was accused of keeping puppets (or "popites") to use in tormenting her victims. This evidence, contained in a deposition given below, caused one modern student of Salem witchcraft to conclude that Bishop was a witch, intent on using magical powers to harm her neighbors. Bishop was the wife of Edward Bishop at the time of her trial and execution, but she had previously been married to a man named Oliver, and the trial records refer to her by both names. These documents are taken from The Salem Witchcraft Papers: Verbatim Transcripts of the Legal Documents of the Salem Witch-craft Outbreak of 1692, *ed. Paul Boyer and Stephen Nissenbaum, (New York, 1977), 1:94–101, 103. Punctuation has been added and abbreviations expanded to clarify meaning.*

Deposition 1: Samuel Gray, May 30, 1692

Samuell Gray of Salem Aged aboute 42 yeares Testifieth and sayth that about fourteen years agoe he goeing to bed well one Lords Day at night, and after he had beene asleep some time, he awak-ened & looking up, saw the house light as if a candle or candles were lighted in it and the dore locked & that little fire there, was Raked up. He did then see a woman standing between the Cradle in the Roome and the Bed side and seemed to look upon him. Soe he did Rise up in his bed and it vanished or disappeared. Then he went to the dore and found it locked. And unlocking and Opening the dore, he went to the Entry dore and looked out, and then againe did see the same Woman he had a little before seene in the Rome [room], and in the same garbe she was in before. Then he said to her "in the name of God what doe you come for?" Then she vanished away. Soe he Locked the dore againe & went to bed. And between sleepeing & wakeing he felt some thing Come to his mouth or lipes cold, & thereupon started & looked up & againe did see the same woman with some thing betweene both her hands holding before [it] his mouth. Upon which she moved. And the Child in the Cradle gave a great screech out as if it was greatly

---

"Depositions," excerpted from *The Salem Witchcraft Papers: Verbatim Tran-scripts of the Legal Documents of the Salem Witchcraft Outbreak of 1692,* Paul Boyer and Stephen Nissenbaum, editors, Harvard University Press, 1977.

hurt. And she [the specter] disappeared. And [he] takeing the child up could not quiett it in some howres. From which tyme, the child that before was a very likely thriveing Child did pine away and was never well, althow it Lived some moneths after, yet in a sad Condition and soe dyed. . . .

Deposition 2: The Reverend John Hale, May 20, 1692

The said Bishop did entertaine people in her house at unseasonable houres in the night, to keep drinking and playing at shovelboard, whereby discord did arise in other families & young people were in danger to bee corrupted &. . . . The said [Christian, wife of John Trask, a neighbor] Trask knew these things & had once gon into the house; & fynding some at shovel-board had taken the peices thay played with & thrown them into the fyre & had reprooved the said Bishop for promoting such disorders, But received no satisfaction from her about it. . . .

But as to Christian Trask, the next news I heard of her was that she was distracted; & asking her husband [John] Trask when she was so taken [he told] mee shee was taken distracted that night after shee [came from] my house when shee complained against Goody Bishop.

She continueing some time Distracted, wee sought the Lord by fasting & prayer & the Lord was pleased to restore the said [Trask] to the use of her reason agen [again]. I was with her often in [her] distraction (& took it then to bee only distraction, yet fearing sometimes somewhat worse). But since I have seen the fitts of those bewitched at Salem Village I call to mind some of hers to be much like some of theirs. . . .

Her distraction (or bewitching) continued about a month and in those intervalls wherein shee was better shee earnestly desired prayers. & the Sabboth before she dyed I received a note for prayers on her behalf which her husband said was written by her selfe; & I judge was her owne hand writing, beeing well acquainted with her hand.

As to the wounds she dyed of, I observed 3 deadly ones; apeice of her wind pipe cutt out. & another wound above that threww the windpipe & Gullet & the veine they call jugular. So that I then judge & still doe apprehend it impossible for her with so short a pair of cissars [scissors] to mangle her selfe so, without some extraordinary work of the devill or witchcraft.

Deposition 3: Samuel Shattock, June 2, 1692

Sundry other tymes she came in a Smooth flattering maner in very Slighty Errants [errands]; we have thought Since [that she did this] on purpos to work mischief. At or very near this tyme our Eldest Child, who promised as much health & understanding both by Countenance and actions as any other Children of his years, was taken in a very drooping Condition. And as She Came oftener to the hous he grew wors & wors. As he would be standing at the door, [he] would fall out & bruis his face upon a great Step Stone, as if he had been thrust out bye an invisible hand, often tymes falling & hitting his face in a very miserable maner. . . .

. . . [H]e grew wors in his fits; and [when he was] out of them, would be allmost allways crying, [so] that for many months he would be crying till nature's strenght was spent & then would fall a sleep and then awake & fall to crying & moaning: that his very Countenance did bespeak Compassion. And at length wee perceived his understanding decayed, Soe that wee feared (as it has Since proved) that he would be quite bereaft of his witts; for Ever Since he has bin Stupified and voide of reason, his fitts still following of him. . . .

Deposition 4: John Louder, June 2, 1692

John Louder of Salem Aged aboute thurtey two Yeares Testifieth and sayth that aboute seaven or Eight years since [ago], I then Liveing with Mr John Gedney in Salem and haveing had some Controversy with Bridgett Bushop the wife of Edward Bushop of Salem, Sawyer [wood finisher], aboate her fowles that used to Come into our orchard or garden. Some little tyme after which, I goeing well to bed, aboute the dead of the night [I] felt a great weight upon my Breast. And awakening [I] looked and, it being bright moonlight, did clearly see said Bridget Bushop or her likeness sitting upon my stomake. . . . [I put] my Armes of[f] of the bed to free myselfe from that great oppression, [but] she presently layd hold of my throat and allmost Choked mee. And I had noe strenth or power in my hands to resist or help my selfe. And in this Condition she held mee to [until] almost day. Some tyme after this, my Mistress Susannah Gedney was in our orchard and I was then with her. And said Bridget Bushop, being then in her Orchard which was next adjoyneing to ours, my Mistress told said Bridget that I said or afirmed that she came one night & satt upon my brest as aforesaid, which she denyed and I afirmed to her face to be true and that I did plainely see her. Upon which discourse with her, she Threatened mee. And some tyme after that I being not very well stayed at home on a Lords day. And on the afternoon of said day, the dores being shutt, I did see a black pig in the Roome Coming towards mee; soe I went towards itt to kick it and it vanished away.

Immediately after I satt down in an Narrow Bar and [I] did see a black thing Jump into the window; and [it] came & stood Just before my face, upon the bar. The body of itt looked like a Munky only the feete ware like a Cocks feete with Claws and the face somewhat more like a mans than a Munkiey. And I being greatly affrighted, not being able to speake or help my selfe by Reason of fear, I suppose; soe the thing spake to mee and said 'I am a Messenger sent to you, for I understand you are trobled in mind, and if you will be Ruled by mee, you shall want for Nothing in this world.' Upon which I endeavored to clap my hands upon itt, and sayd 'You devill I will Kill you.' But I could feale noe substance. . . .

I Againe did see that or the like creture that I before did see within dores, in such a posture as it seemed to be agoeing to fly at mee. Upon which I cryed out: 'the whole armor of god be between mee and you.' Soe itt sprang back and flew over the apple tree, flinging the dust with its feet against my stomake. Upon which I was struck dumb, and soe Continued for aboute three days tyme. And also shook many of the apples of[f] from the tree which it flu over.

Deposition 5: John Bly, Sr., and William Bly, June 2, 1692

Jno Blye Senior aged about 57 years & William Blye aged about 15 years both of Salem Testifieth and sayth that, being Imployed by Bridgitt Bushup Alies Oliver of Salem to help take downe the Cellar wall of The owld house she formerly Lived in, wee the said Deponants, in holes of the said owld wall Belonging to the said sellar, found Severall popitts made up of Raggs And hoggs Brusells with headles pins in Them, with the points out ward & this was about Seaven years Last past.

Deposition 6: John Bly, Sr., and Rebecca Bly, no date

Jno Bly Bought a Sow of Edward Bushop of Salem . . . and Bridgett, the wife of Said Edward Bushop, because she could not have the mony or vallue agreed for, payd unto her, she [came] to the house of the deponents in Salem and Quarrelled with them aboute it. Soon after which the sow haveing piged, she was taken with strange fitts, Jumping up and knocking hir head against the fence and seemed blind and deafe and would not Eat neither Lett her pigs suck, but foamed at the mouth . . . wee did then Apprehend or Judge & doe still that said Bishop had bewitched said sow.

Bringing the Witch Trials to an End

Increase Mather, the leading minister in the colony in 1692, returned from London, where he had been negotiating a new charter for the Massachusetts government, and confronted the witch scare. After observing the proceedings for a time, he joined with other ministers to produce the statement reprinted below. The effect of their declaration was to bring the trials to a halt, since in it the ministers questioned the judges' use of evidence. Whereas the judges were willing to believe that the appearance of one's specter proved that one was a witch, the ministers suggested that the devil might cause an innocent person's likeness to appear as a way to bring charges down on the godly. Because ministers were experts on the theological questions raised by witchcraft prosecutions, their opinions mattered to the governor and his council, to whom this statement was addressed. This document was printed in Increase Mather's Cases of Conscience *(Boston, 1693), unpaginated appendix.*

The Return of several Ministers consulted by his Excellency, and the Honourable Council, upon the present Witchcrafts in *Salem* Village.

Boston, June 15. 1692

I. The afflicted State of our poor Neighbours, that are now suffering by Molestations from the Invisible World, we apprehend so deplorable, that we think their Condition calls for the utmost help of all Persons in their several Capacities.

II. We cannot but with all Thankfulness acknowledge, the Success which the merciful God has given unto the sedulous and assiduous Endeavors of our honourable Rulers, to detect the abominable Witchcrafts which have been committed in the Country; humbly *praying that the discovery of these mysterious and mischievous Wickednesses, may be perfected.*

III. We judge that in the prosecution of these, and all such Witchcrafts, there is need of a very critical and exquisite Caution, left by too much Credulity for things received only upon the Devil's Authority, there be a Door opened for a long Train of miserable Consequences, and Satan get an Advantage over us, for we should not be ignorant of his Devices.

IV. . . .'tis necessary that all Proceedings thereabout be managed with an exceeding tenderness toward those that may be complained of; especially if they have been Persons formerly of an unblemished Reputation.

V. When the first Enquiry is made into the Circumstances of such as may lie under any just Suspicion of Witchcrafts, we could wish that there may be admitted as little as is possible, of such Noise, Company, and Openness, as may too hastily expose them that are examined; and that there may nothing be used as a Test, for the Trial of the suspected, the Lawfulness whereof may be doubted among the People of God; but that the Directions given by such Judicious Writers as Perkins and Bernard, be consulted in such a Case.

At the close of his pamphlet opposing the witch trials, Increase Mather added a postscript protesting that he did not want to be misunderstood. In particular, Mather feared that readers might think he did not believe in witches or that he intended to criticize the trial judges. These excerpts from his postscript reveal how uncomfortable New England elites felt about publishing their differences; in addition they suggest that Mather did not want to be seen as contributing to irreligion by denying again the existence of the supernatural.

The Design of the preceding *Dissertation,* is not to plead for Witchcrafts, or to appear as an Advocate for Witches: I have therefore written another Discourse proving that there are such horrid Creatures as Witches in the World; and that they are to be extripated and cut off from amongst the People of God, which I have Thoughts and Inclinations in due time to publish; and I am abundantly satisfied that there have been, and are still most cursed Witches in the Land. More then one or two of those now in

Prison, have freely and credibly acknowledged their Communion and Familiarity with the Spirits of Darkness; and have also declared unto me the Time and Occasion, with the particular Circumstances of their Hellish Obligations and Abominations.

Nor is there designed any Reflection on those worthy Persons who have been concerned in the late Proceedings at *Salam:* They are wise and good Men, and have acted with all Fidelity according to their Light, and have out of tenderness declined the doing of some things, which in our own Judgments they were satisfied about: Having therefore so arduous a Case before them, Pitty and Prayers rather than Censures are their due; on which account I am glad that there is published to the World (by my Son) a *Breviate of the Tryals* of some who were lately executed, whereby I hope the thinking part of Mankind will be satisfied, that there was more than that which is called *Spectre Evidence* for the Conviction of the Persons condemned.

Cotton Mather Assesses the Witch Trials

In the following passage, Cotton Mather—also a Boston minister like his father, Increase Mather—addresses three questions. First, what had been the principle evidence in the witch trials; second, what led him to conclude that the trials went too far; and, third, what were the most serious mistakes made at Salem? Note that Mather, like his father, continued to believe that Satan works evil in the world through witches, even as he suggests that witches may not have been the source of the problem in this particular case. The following is taken from Mather's monumental history of early New England, Magnalia Christi Americana *(1702); this excerpt was taken from the 1820 edition, 2:413–14.*

By these things you may see how this matter was carry'd on, *viz.* chiefly by the complaints and accusations of the afflicted (bewitch'd ones, as it was suppos'd) and then by the confessions of the *accus'd* condemning themselves and others. Yet experience shew'd, that the more there were apprehended, the more were still afflicted by satan; and the number of confessors increasing, did but increase the number of the *accused;* and the executing of

Cotton Mather (1663–1728) was a clergyman in one of the Boston churches in 1692. Because he had previously assisted with the case of a girl who was apparently bewitched, he was considered something of an expert on the supernatural. In this, he followed in the footsteps of his powerful and important father, Increase Mather who—along with Cotton and other ministers—helped to bring the trials to an end (Courtesy of the New York Public Library.)

some, made way for the apprehending of others: For still the afflicted complain'd of being tormented by new objects, as the former were remov'd. So that those that were concern'd, grew amaz'd at the number and quality of the persons accus'd, and feared that satan by his wiles had enwrapped innocent persons under the imputation of that crime. And at last, it was evidently seen, that there must be a stop put, or the generation of the children of God, would fall under that condemnation. Henceforth therefore the juries generally acquitted such as were tried, fearing they had gone too far before. And Sir *William Phips* the Governour, repriev'd all that were condemn'd, even the confessors as well as others. And the confessors generally fell off from their confession, some saying, *They remembred nothing of what they had said;* others said, *They had belied themselves and others.* Some broke prison and ran away, and were not strictly searched after. Some acquitted, some dismissed, and one way or other, all that had been accused, were set or left at liberty. . . .

It may be queried, How doth it appear that there was a going too far in this *affair?*

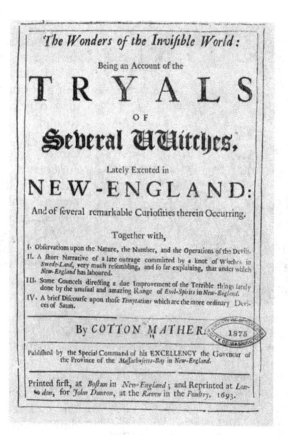

The Wonders of the Invisible World:

Being an Account of the

T R Y A L S

O F

𝕾𝖊𝖛𝖊𝖗𝖆𝖑 𝖂𝖆𝖎𝖙𝖈𝖍𝖊𝖘,

Lately Executed in

N E W - E N G L A N D:

And of feveral remarkable Curiofities therein Occurring.

Together with,

I. Obfervations upon the Nature, the Number, and the Operations of the Devils.

II. A fhort Narrative of a late outrage committed by a knot of Witches in *Sweds-Land*, very much refembling, and fo far explaining, that under which *New-England* has laboured.

III. Some Councels directing a due Improvement of the Terrible things lately done by the unufual and amazing Range of *Evil-Spirits* in *New-England.*

IV. A brief Difcourfe upon thofe *Temptations* which are the more ordinary Devices of Satan.

By *COTTON MATHER.* 1875

Publifhed by the Special Command of his EXCELLENCY the Governour of the Province of the *Maffachufetts-Bay* in *New-England.*

Printed firft, at *Bofton* in *New-England* ; and Reprinted at *London*, for *John Dunton*, at the *Raven* in the *Poultry*. 1693.

Title page to Cotton Mather, The Wonders of the Invisible World *(London, 1693). Mather, who had grave reservations about the work of the court that tried the witchcraft cases in 1692, nonetheless felt compelled to defend it against critics. His account, contained in this pamphlet, reveals his conflicted attitudes. The title of his pamphlet refers back to an early work by his father, Increase Mather, that argued in favor of "an invisible world" against skeptics. (Courtesy of the Library of Congress.)*

By the numbers of the persons accus'd, which at length increas'd to about an hundred; and it cannot be imagin'd that in a place of so much knowledge, so many in so small a compass of land, should so abominably leap into the devil's lap all at once.

The quality of several of the accus'd was such, as did bespeak *better things, and things that accompany salvation;* Persons, whose blameless and holy lives before did testifie for them; Persons that had taken great pains to bring up their children in the nurture and admonition of the Lord; such as we had charity for, as for our own souls: And charity is a christian duty commended to us.

The number of the afflicted daily increased until about fifty persons were thus vex'd by the devil. This gave just ground to suspect some mistake, which gave advantage to the *accuser of the brethren* to make a breach upon us.

It was considerable, that *nineteen* were executed, and all denied the crime to the death, and some of them were knowing persons, and had before this been accounted blameless *livers*. . . .

When this prosecution ceas'd, the Lord so *chain'd up satan,* that the afflicted grew presently well: The accused are generally quiet; and for five years since, we have no such molestation by them.

It sways much with me, which I have since heard and read, of the like mistakes in other places. As in Suffolk in England, about the year 1645 was such a prosecution, until they saw, that unless they put a stop, it would bring all into blood and confusion. The like hath been in France, until nine hundred were put to death. And in some other places the like So that New-England is not the only place circumvented by the *wiles of the wicked and wily serpent in this kind.* . . .

As to our case at *Salem,* I conceive it proceeded from some mistaken principles: As, that satan cannot assume the shape of an innocent person, and in that shape do mischief to the bodies and estates of mankind: and that the devil, when he doth harm to persons in their body or estate, it is (at least, most commonly, generally and frequently) by the help of our neighbour, some witch in covenant with the devil; and that when the party suspected looks on the parties suppos'd to be bewitch'd, and they are thereupon struck down into a fit, as if struck with a cudgel, it is a proof of such a covenant.

Questions

1. If they continued to believe in the existence of witchcraft, how did various leading colonists come to oppose the trials?
2. What do the depositions reveal about popular attitudes regarding witches?
3. Can you see any differences between lay and clerical thinking when you compare the depositions and the ministers' statements?

FURTHER READING

The most popular book on Salem witchcraft among undergraduates remains Salem Possessed: The Social Origins of Witchcraft, *by Paul Boyer and Stephen Nissenbaum (Cambridge, Massachusetts, 1974).* John Putnam Demos's Entertaining Satan: Witchcraft and the Culture of Early New England *(New York, 1982) and Carol Karlsen's* The Devil in the Shape of a Woman: Witchcraft in Colonial New England *(New York, 1987) examine the Salem accusations in the context of the long history of witch fears in colonial New England. The* Devil's Dominion: Magic and Religion in Early New England *(New York, 1992), by Richard Godbeer, includes two chapters on Salem. Trial transcripts are available in* The Salem Witchcraft Papers: Verbatim Transcripts of the Legal Documents of the Salem Witchcraft Outbreak of 1692, *ed. Paul Boyer and Stephen Nissenbaum, 3 vols. (New York, 1977); other original documents can be found in* Witch-hunting in Seventeenth-Century New England: A Documentary History, 1638–1692, *ed. David D. Hall (Boston, 1991).*

The Albany Plan of Union

During the early 1750s, tensions over territorial claims in North America between France and Great Britain increased. The land under dispute was the Ohio River Valley, stretching into present-day western Pennsylvania. Skirmishes between British troops, led by a young George Washington, and French troops continued in 1754, prompting the British government to call for a meeting of delegates from Virginia and all colonies north of it as well as from the powerful Iroquois Confederacy. While its main concern was ensuring a unified colonial defense, solidifying good relations with the Iroquois Confederacy was also important. However, at the meeting, the Iroquois representatives refused to make a definitive pledge of support for the British.

This meeting, held from June 19 to July 10, 1754, yielded few concrete results, with the exception of the proposed Albany Plan of Union. The chief drafters of this plan were Benjamin Franklin and Thomas Hutchinson, future Governor of Massachusetts. Its purpose was to establish a centralized government for the British colonies in North America, with power resting in an executive (President General) appointed by the monarch of Great Britain and a grand council, composed of forty-eight members chosen by colonial legislatures. These representatives were to serve three-year terms, meeting at least once a year in a regular session; they could also be called into an emergency session by the executive. Although the delegates to the Albany Congress approved the plan, both the colonial legislatures and the British government rejected it. What powers did the Plan of Union propose that this new government should have? Why did the British government reject the Plan? Why did colonial legislatures also disapprove of it?

From *Documents of American History*, ed. Henry Steele Commager, F. S. Crofts & Co., (New York, 1947), copyright © 1934, 1940, 1943 by F. S. Crofts & Co. Inc. 43–45.

Albany Plan of Union 1754

It is proposed that humble application be made for an act of Parliament of Great Britain, by virtue of which one general government may be formed in America, including all the said colonies, within and under which government each colony may retain its present constitution, except in the particulars wherein a change may be directed by the said act, as hereafter follows.

1. That the said general government be administered by a President-General, to be appointed and supported by the crown; and a Grand Council, to be chosen by the representatives of the people of the several Colonies met in their respective assemblies.

2. That within__months after the passing such act, the House of Representatives that happen to be sitting within that time, or that shall especially for that purpose convened, may and shall choose members for the Grand Council, in the following proportion, that is to say: Massachusetts Bay 7, New Hampshire 2, Connecticut 5, Rhode Island 2, New York 4, New Jersey 3, Pennsylvania 6, Maryland 4, Virginia 7, North Carolina 4, South Carolina 4.

. . .

5. That after the first three years, when the proportion of money arising out of each Colony to the general treasury can be known, the number of members to be chosen for each Colony shall, from time to time, in all ensuing elections, be regulated by that proportion, yet so as that the number to be chosen by any one Province be not more than seven, nor less than two.

. . .

8. That the members of the Grand Council shall be allowed for their service ten shillings sterling per diem, during their session and journey to and from the place of meeting; twenty miles to be reckoned a day's journey.

9. That the assent of the President-General be requisite to all acts of the Grand Council, and that it be his office and duty to cause them to be carried into execution.

10. That the President-General, with the advice of the Grand Council, hold or direct all Indian treaties, in which the general

interest of the Colonies may be concerned; and make peace or declare war with Indian nations.

11. That they make such laws as they judge necessary for regulating all Indian trade.

12. That they make all purchases from Indians, for the crown, of lands not now within the bounds of particular Colonies, or that shall not be within their bounds when some of them are reduced to more convenient dimensions.

. . .

15. That they raise and pay soldiers and build forts for the defense of any of the Colonies, and equip vessels of force to guard the coasts and protect the trade on the ocean, lakes, or great rivers; but they shall not impress men in any Colony, without the consent of the Legislature.

16. That for these purposes they have power to make laws, and lay and levy such general duties, imposts, or taxes, as to them shall appear most equal and just (considering the ability and other circumstances of the inhabitants in the several Colonies), and such as may be collected with the least inconvenience to the people; rather discouraging luxury, than loading industry with unnecessary burdens.

. . .

20. That a quorum of the Grand Council, empowered to act with the President-General, do consist of twenty-five members; among whom there shall be one or more from a majority of the Colonies.

21. That the laws made by them for the purposes aforesaid shall not be repugnant, but, as near as may be, agreeable to the laws of England, and shall be transmitted to the King in Council for approbation, as soon as may be after their passing; and if not disapproved within three years after presentation, to remain in force.

. . .

25. That the particular military as well as civil establishments in each Colony remain in their present state, the general constitution notwithstanding; and that on sudden emergencies any Colony may defend itself, and lay the accounts of expense thence arising before the President-General and General Council, who may allow and order payment of the same, as far as they judge such accounts just and reasonable

Federalist #10

Virginia planter James Madison drafted the plan that formed the basis of the federal Constitution. He also emerged as one of the Constitution's most effective advocates during the struggle over ratification. In late 1787, Madison joined forces with two other prominent Federalists, John Jay and Alexander Hamilton, to defend his creation against anti-Federalist attacks. The three collaborated on a series of eighty-five essays that first appeared in New York newspapers and were republished under the title of The Federalist Papers. *Among Madison's contributions, his most famous is "Federalist No. 10," which historians and political scientists today still regard as a classic statement of American constitutional principles. In the essay, he took aim at the inherited belief that a republican system of government was only viable on a small scale. Standing this argument on its head, Madison asserted that size was actually an asset. In a large republic, the multitude of factions and divisions that naturally arose in any society would cancel one another out, thus ensuring that no one group could tyrannize the others. Equally important, the government of a large republic would be less likely to fall under the influence of special interests and so would be more capable of exercising its authority in a manner that promoted the common good for all people.*

November 22, 1787

To the People of the State of New York

Among the numerous advantages promised by a well-constructed Union, none deserves to be more accurately developed than its tendency to break and control the violence of faction. . . . Complaints are everywhere heard from our most considerate and virtuous citizens, equally the friends of public and

---

From James Madison, "Federalist No. 10," in *The Federalist: A Commentary on the Constitution of the United States,* ed. Paul Leicester Ford, (New York, 1898), 54–60, 62–63.

private faith and of public and personal liberty, that our governments are too unstable, that the public good is disregarded in the conflicts of rival parties, and that measures are too often decided, not according to the rules of justice and the rights of the minor party, but by the superior force of an interested and overbearing majority. . . .

By a faction I understand a number of citizens, whether amounting to a majority or minority of the whole, who are united and actuated by some common impulse of passion, or of interest, adverse to the rights of other citizens, or to the permanent and aggregate interests of the community. . . .

There are again two methods of removing the causes of faction: the one, by destroying the liberty which is essential to its existence; the other, by giving to every citizen the same opinions, the same passions, and the same interests. . . .

The latent causes of faction are thus sown in the nature of man; and we see them everywhere brought into different degrees of activity, according to the different circumstances of civil society. A zeal for different opinions concerning religion, concerning government, and many other points, as well of speculation as of practice; an attachment to different leaders ambitiously contending for pre-eminence and power; or to persons of other descriptions whose fortunes have been interesting to the human passions, have, in turn, divided mankind into parties, inflamed them with mutual animosity, and rendered them much more disposed to vex and oppress each other than to co-operate for their common good. . . . But the most common and durable source of factions has been the various and unequal distribution of property. Those who hold and those who are without property have ever formed distinct interests in society. Those who are creditors, and those who are debtors, fall under a like discrimination. A landed interest, a manufacturing interest, a mercantile interest, a moneyed interest, with many lesser interests, grow up of necessity in civilized nations, and divide them into different classes actuated by different sentiments and views. The regulation of these various and interfering interests forms the principal task of modern legislation and involves the spirit of party and faction in the necessary and ordinary operations of the government. . . .

It is in vain to say that enlightened statesmen will be able to adjust these clashing interests and render them all subservient to the public good. Enlightened statesmen will not always be at the helm. . . .

The inference to which we are brought is that the *causes* of faction cannot be removed and that relief is only to be sought in the means of controlling its *effects*. . . .

By what means is this object attainable? Evidently by one of two only: Either the existence of the same passion or interest in a majority at the same time must be prevented, or the majority, having such coexistent passion or interest, must be rendered, by their number and local situation, unable to concert and carry into effect schemes of oppression. . . .

From this view of the subject it may be concluded that a pure democracy, by which I mean a society consisting of a small number of citizens, who assemble and administer the government in person, can admit of no cure for the mischiefs of faction. . . . Hence it is that such democracies have ever been spectacles of turbulence and contention; have ever been found incompatible with personal security or the rights of property; and have in general been as short in their lives as they have been violent in their deaths. . . .

A republic, by which I mean a government in which the scheme of representation takes place, opens a different prospect and promises the cure for which we are seeking. Let us examine the points in which it varies from pure democracy, and we shall comprehend both the nature of the cure and the efficacy which it must derive from the Union.

The two great points of difference between a democracy and a republic are: first, the delegation of the government in the latter, to a small number of citizens elected by the rest; secondly, the greater number of citizens and greater sphere of country over which the latter may be extended.

The effect of the first difference is, on the one hand, to refine and enlarge the public views by passing them through the medium of a chosen body of citizens, whose wisdom may best discern the true interest of their country and whose patriotism and love of justice will be least likely to sacrifice it to temporary or partial considerations. . . .

The other point of difference is the greater number of citizens and extent of territory which may be brought within the compass of republican than of democratic government; and it is this circumstance principally which renders factious combinations less to be dreaded in the former than in the latter. The smaller the society, the fewer probably will be the distinct parties and interests composing it; the fewer the distinct parties and interests, the more frequently will a majority be found of the same party; and the smaller the number of individuals composing a majority, and the smaller the compass within which they are placed, the more easily will they concert and execute their plans of oppression. Extend the sphere and you take in a greater variety of parties and interests; you make it less probable that a majority of the whole will have a common motive to invade the rights of other citizens; or if such a common motive exists, it will be more difficult for all who feel it to discover their own strength and to act in unison with each other. . . .

The influence of factious leaders may kindle a flame within their particular States but will be unable to spread a general conflagration through the other States. A religious sect may degenerate into a political faction in a part of the Confederacy; but the variety of sects dispersed over the entire face of it must secure the national councils against any danger from that source. A rage for paper money, for an abolition of debts, for an equal division of property, or for any other improper or wicked project, will be less apt to pervade the whole body of the Union than a particular member of it, in the same proportion as such a malady is more likely to taint a particular county or district than an entire State.

In the extent and proper structure of the Union, therefore, we behold a republican remedy for the diseases most incident to republican government. . . .

PUBLIUS.

Final Report of the Hartford Convention

On June 1, 1812, President James Madison called for military action against Great Britain. Tensions had been building for years as the British impressed American seamen into the Royal Navy, violated American neutrality rights through trade restrictions, and allied with Native Americans on the turbulent Northwest frontier. From 1807 to 1812, the United States had tried to resolve disagreements with Britain peacefully, but the British continued to violate U.S. rights. Despite a decade of provocation, Madison's declaration of war still faced substantial opposition in Congress. New England, the last bastion of the dying Federalist Party, and the Middle Atlantic states generally opposed the war. American merchants might be angered by British policies, but they still made money by supplying British armies fighting against the French in Europe.

As the War of 1812 progressed, Federalist leaders hampered Madison by taking a strong states' right approach and a narrow view of the Constitution. Federalists' activism culminated in a wartime convention at Hartford, Connecticut, in which the party came close to treason by passing resolutions censuring Republican practices and suggesting a series of amendments to the U.S. Constitution to safeguard against their recurrence. The convention expected to meet after Congress responded to their demands, but the war ended and, lacking public support, so did the Federalist Party. The final report of the convention, approved in January 1815, appears below.

The convention is deeply impressed with a sense of the arduous nature of the commission which they were appointed to execute, of devising the means of defence against dangers, and of relief from oppressions proceeding from the acts of their own government, without violating constitutional principles, or disap-

From *History of the Hartford Convention*, by Theodore Dwight, (New York, 1833), 352–355, 362–363, 365.

pointing the hopes of a suffering and injured people. . . . Necessity alone can sanction a resort to this measure; and it should never be extended in duration or degree beyond the exigency, until the people, not merely in the fervour of sudden excitement, but after full deliberation, are determined to change the constitution.

It is a truth, not to be concealed, that a sentiment prevails to no inconsiderable extent, that administration have given such constructions to that instrument, and practised so many abuses under colour of its authority, that the time for a change is at hand. . . .

Although this high state of public happiness has undergone a miserable and afflicting reverse, through the prevalence of a weak and profligate policy, yet the evils and afflictions which have thus been induced upon the country, are not peculiar to any form of government. The lust and caprice of power, the corruption of patronage, the oppression of the weaker interests of the community by the stronger, heavy taxes, wasteful expenditures, and unjust and ruinous wars, are the natural offspring of bad administrations, in all ages and countries. It was indeed to be hoped, that the rulers of these states would not make such disastrous haste to involve their infancy in the embarrassments of old and rotten institutions. Yet all this have they done; and their conduct calls loudly for their dismission and disgrace. But to attempt upon every abuse of power to change the constitution, would be to perpetuate the evils of revolution.

Again, the experiment of the powers of the constitution to regain its vigour, and of the people to recover from their delusions, has been hitherto made under the greatest possible disadvantages arising from the state of the world. The fierce passions which have convulsed the nations of Europe, have passed the ocean, and finding their way to the bosoms of our citizens, have afforded to administration the means of perverting public opinion, in respect to our foreign relations, so as to acquire its aid in the indulgence of their animosities, and the increase of their adherents. Further, a reformation of public opinion, resulting from dear-bought experience, in the southern Atlantic states, at least, is not to be despaired of. They will have felt, that the eastern states cannot be made exclusively the victims of a capricious and impassioned policy. They will have seen that the great and essential interests of the people are common to the south and to the east. They will realize the fatal errors of a system which seeks revenge for commercial injuries in the sacrifice of commerce, and aggravates by needless wars, to an immeasurable extent, the injuries it professes to redress. They may discard the influence of visionary theorists, and recognize the benefits of a practical policy. . . .

In the prosecution of this favourite warfare, administration have left the exposed and vulnerable parts of the country destitute of all the efficient means of defence. The main body of the regular army has been marched to the frontier. The navy has been stripped of a great part of its sailors for the service of the lakes. Meanwhile the enemy scours the sea-coast, blockades our ports, ascends our bays and rivers, makes actual descents in various and distant places, holds some by force, and threatens all that are assailable with fire and sword. The sea-board of four of the New-England states, following its curvatures, presents an extent of more than seven hundred miles, generally occupied by a compact population, and accessible by a naval force, exposing a mass of people and property to the devastation of the enemy, which bears a great proportion to the residue of the maritime frontier of the United States. This extensive shore has been exposed to frequent attacks, repeated contributions, and constant alarms. The regular forces detached by the national government for its defence are mere pretexts for placing officers of high rank in command. They are besides confined to a few places, and are too insignificant in number to be included in any computation. . . .

. . . When a great and brave people shall feel themselves deserted by their government, and reduced to the necessity either of submission to a foreign enemy, or of appropriating to their own use those means of defence which are indispensable to self-preservation, they cannot consent to wait passive spectators of approaching ruin, which it is in their power to avert, and to resign the last remnant of their industrious earnings to be dissipated in support of measures destructive of the best interests of the nation.

This convention will not trust themselves to express their conviction of the catastrophe to which such a state of things inevitably tends. Conscious of their high responsibility to God and their country, solicitous for the continuance of the Union, as well as the sovereignty of the states, unwilling to furnish obstacles to peace— resolute never to submit to a foreign enemy, and confiding in the Divine care and protection, they will, until the last hope shall be extinguished, endeavor to avert such consequences.

The Trek Across the Continent

In order to both chart the vast acreage of the Louisiana Purchase and establish diplomatic contact with (and, as the United States understood it, sovereignty over) the various Native American societies therein, President Thomas Jefferson proposed to Congress in 1803 the creation of a scientific and political expedition to follow the Missouri River to its source and, if possible, pass across the Continental Divide to the Pacific Ocean. The Corps of Discovery—known more commonly as the Lewis and Clark Expedition—was the nineteenth century equivalent, in its perceived levels of physical danger and nationalist glory, of both the expeditions of Spanish explorers like Coronado and De Leon, and of the Apollo space program of the 1960s.

Today's knowledge of the journeys of Lewis and Clark comes primarily from their own journals of the expedition. These extraordinary journals—and the Lewis and Clark expedition generally—exhibit many different facets of America's collective identity at the turn of the nineteenth century. They are part travel epic, part scientific and anthropological treatise, part official government report, and part adventure story; they are simultaneously a tribute to and an assault on Nature, a tale of both honest diplomacy and imperialist intrigue, and an exercise in both Enlightenment rationalism and Romantic heroism.

[Clark], 1 January 1805

The Day was ushered in by the Descharge of two Cannon, we Suffered 16 men with their Musick to visit the 1st Village for the purpose of Danceing, by as they Said the perticular request of the Chiefs of that Village. About 11 oClock I with an inturpeter & two men walked up to the Village, (my views were to alay Some little

---

From *The Journals of Lewis and Clark,* by Bernard DeVoto, (Boston, 1953), 75, 108–109, 118, 171.

Miss understanding which had taken place thro jelloucy and mortification as to our treatment towards them.) I found them much pleased at the Danceing of our men. I ordered my black Servent to Dance which amused the Croud Verry much, and Somewhat astonished them, that So large a man should be active &c. . . .

[Lewis], 14 May 1805

. . . In the evening, the men in two of the rear canoes discovered a large brown bear lying in the open grounds about 300 paces from the river, and six of them went out to attack him, all good hunters; they took the advantage of a small eminence which concealed them and got within 40 paces of him, unperceived. Two of them reserved their fires as had been previously conserted, the four others fired nearly at the same time and put each his bullet through him, two of the balls passed through the bulk of both lobes of his lungs. In an instant this monster ran at them with open mouth, the two who had reserved their fir[e]s discharged their pieces at him as he came towards them, boath of them struck him, one only slightly and the other fortunately broke his shoulder. This however only retarded his motion for a moment. The men unable to reload their guns took to flight, the bear pursued and had very nearly overtaken them before they reached the river; two of the party betook themselves to a canoe and the others seperated an[d] concealed themselves among the willows, reloaded their pieces, each discharged his piece at him as they had an opportunity. They struck him several times again but the guns served only to direct the bear to them. In this manner he pursued two of them seperately so close that they were obliged to throw aside their guns and pouches and throw themselves into the river altho' the bank was nearly twenty feet perpendicular. So enraged was this anamal that he plunged into the river only a few feet behind the second man he had compelled [to] take refuge in the water, when one of those who still remained on shore shot him through the head and finally killed him. They then took him ashore and butch[er]ed him when they found eight balls had passed through him in different directions. The bear being old the flesh was indifferent, they therefore only took the skin and fleece, the latter made us several gallons of oil. . . .

[Lewis], 26 May 1805

. . . I beheld the Rocky Mountains for the first time. . . . [W]hile I viewed these mountains I felt a secret pleasure in finding myself so near the head of the heretofore conceived boundless Missouri; but when I reflected on the difficulties which this snowey barrier would most probably throw in my way to the Pacific, and the sufferings and hardships of myself and party in thim, it in some measure counterballanced the joy I had felt in the first moments in which I gazed on them; but as I have always held it a crime to anticipate evils I will believe it a good comfortable road untill I am compelled to believe differently. . . .

[Lewis], 28 July 1805, at the three forks of the Missouri

. . . Our present camp is precisely on the spot . . . [where] the Minnetarees . . . killed 4 men 4 women a number of boys, and mad[e] prisoners of all the females and four boys. *Sah-cah-gar-we-ah* o[u]r Indian woman was one of the female prisoners taken at that time; tho' I cannot discover that she shews any immotion of sorrow in recollecting this event, or of joy in being restored to her native country; if she has enough to eat and a few trinkets to wear I believe she would be perfectly content anywhere.

The Gettysburg Address

The Battle of Gettysburg (July 1–3, 1863) was the bloodiest battle of the American Civil War. At Gettysburg, the Union army scored a great victory and turned the tide of the war. On November 19, 1863, President Abraham Lincoln participated in the dedication of the national cemetery at Gettysburg. In a speech that lasted only three minutes, Lincoln declared that the fundamental objective of the war was to defend freedom and secure equality for all men. Although Lincoln never explicitly mentioned slavery, he clearly affirmed that the destruction of the "peculiar institution" was the moral purpose behind the Union war effort.

Fourscore and seven years ago our fathers brought forth on this continent a new nation, conceived in liberty, and dedicated to the proposition that all men are created equal.

Now we are engaged in a great civil war, testing whether that nation, or any nation so conceived and so dedicated, can long endure. We are met on a great battle-field of that war. We have come to dedicate a portion of that field as a final resting-place for those who here gave their lives that that nation might live. It is altogether fitting and proper that we should do this.

But, in a larger sense, we cannot dedicate—we cannot consecrate—we cannot hallow—this ground. The brave men, living and dead, who struggled here, have consecrated it far above our poor power to add or detract. The world will little note nor long remember what we say here, but it can never forget what they did here. It is for us, the living, rather, to be dedicated here to the unfinished work which they who fought here have thus far so nobly advanced. It is rather for us to be here dedicated to the great

From *Abraham Lincoln: Complete Works Comprising His Speeches, Letters, State Papers, and Miscellaneous Writings: Volume 2*, ed. John G. Nicolay and John Hay, The Century Co., (New York, 1894), 439.

task remaining before us—that from these honored dead we take increased devotion to that cause for which they gave the last full measure of devotion; that we here highly resolve that these dead shall not have died in vain; that this nation, under God, shall have a new birth of freedom; and that the government of the people, by the people, for the people, shall not perish from the earth.

The Struggle for
Black Rights
during Reconstruction

Michael Les Benedict

INTRODUCTION

The Civil War and Reconstruction era witnessed a desperate fight for equal civil and political rights for African Americans. The legal position of black Americans had deteriorated in the first part of the nineteenth century, with racism actually growing in the North and South as slavery was rejuvenated by the development of cotton agriculture. The growth of the antislavery movement in the 1840s and 1850s, however, led some Northerners to argue that African Americans were entitled to the rights of citizenship. The Supreme Court's Dred Scott decision was a watershed that dashed black Americans' claims to citizenship. Black hopes and expectations brightened with the passage of the Thirteenth Amendment, but they were dimmed once more by the adoption of restrictive southern Black Codes. Seeing the codes as an attempt to salvage key aspects of slavery, Republicans urged the passage of the Civil Rights Act of 1866 to ensure that all Americans, regardless of color, received the basic rights of citizenship. Congress passed the bill, only to be rebuffed by President Andrew Johnson's veto. Overriding the president's veto, Republicans then passed the Fourteenth Amendment in an effort to secure African-American citizenship and rights beyond constitutional doubt.

While blacks embraced their new citizenship, they continued to demand suffrage. Among the most eloquent was Frederick Douglass, one of the greatest orators of his day. The clamor for black enfranchisement aroused apprehension among southern whites that black voters might overturn the traditional social order. The white people of Alabama were among those who voiced their fears of black dominance in a petition to Congress. Nonethe-

less, Congress imposed black suffrage on the South in the Reconstruction Act of 1867, and in 1870 the requisite number of states ratified the Fifteenth Amendment, which extended the change throughout the nation and made it permanent.

But Republicans proved unable to secure equal civil and political rights for African Americans over bitter southern white resistance. A series of Supreme Court decisions narrowed the definition of federal citizenship and limited Congress's power to protect these rights. The court proclaimed that the postwar constitutional amendments authorized the federal government to protect rights only against violations by state authorities, leaving African Americans to rely on unsympathetic state and local officials to protect them against all other invasions of their rights.

SECURING EQUAL RIGHTS: THE DOCUMENTARY RECORD

As slaves, most African Americans had been denied nearly all fundamental rights. But for much of the time before the Civil War, the civil status of free African Americans was uncertain. Many Northern states considered them citizens entitled to basic rights; most of the New England states conceded them political rights as well. Other states denied or limited the basic rights of free blacks to travel, to associate with others, and to sue and testify in court, without making clear whether they were citizens or not. It was uncertain how state citizenship related to United States citizenship. Not until the case of Dred Scott v. Sandford did the Supreme Court answer that question. In this case, the Supreme Court distinguished United States citizenship from state citizenship and held that African Americans were not citizens of the United States, whether they were citizens of individual states or not.

White southerners refused to accept the legitimacy of state governments elected by black voters, and they engaged in systematic violence to resubordinate African Americans and to paralyze the Republican state officials in the South. From 1868 to 1871 much of the violence was instigated by the Ku Klux Klan, loosely organized gangs of white terrorists that sprang up in various southern localities. From 1874 to 1876 the Democratic party organized "White Leagues," "Red Shirts," and less formal armed auxiliaries to break up the Republican party. Both white and black Republicans were victimized.

Most of the southern states passed vagrancy laws that prohibited freedpeople from buying or leasing land or homes, except in towns, and then authorized towns to make their own regulations.

The following documents will introduce you to the legislation and arguments associated with the effort to secure equal rights after the Civil War, as well as to the practical effect on the lives of ordinary people. Read them in light of the questions that follow this section, particularly considering how far Republicans intended to change the American system of government in order to protect citizens' rights.

The Thirteenth Amendment

Congress passed the Thirteenth Amendment in January 1865 and it was ratified by December of that same year. The amendment abolished slavery throughout the United States.

Section 1 - Neither slavery nor involuntary servitude, except as a punishment for crime whereof the party shall have been duly convicted, shall exist within the United States, or any place subject to their jurisdiction.

Section 2 - Congress shall have power to enforce this article by appropriate legislation.

The Black Codes

Under President Andrew Johnson's plan of reconstruction, southern state governments, elected by white men who had taken an oath pledging loyalty to the United States, passed laws specifying the rights of the freedpeople. Some were more restrictive than others. All gave freedpeople the right to make contracts and to buy, own, and sell property. Some subjected them to the same criminal laws and punishments that covered white people; others subjected them to the harsher criminal laws that had covered free black people before the war. None of the codes extended political rights or the right to serve on juries. Local communities also passed regulations that limited freedpeople's rights. The following are examples of restrictive state and local provisions that convinced Republicans to intervene.

Selections from the Mississippi Black Code conferring civil rights on freedmen and defining vagrancy are from Laws of the State of Mississippi . . . *(1866), 82-84, 91 92.*

Mississippi Black Code

An Act to confer Civil Rights on Freedmen . . .

Section 1. . . . [A]ll freedmen, free negroes and mulattoes may sue and be sued . . . in all the courts of law and equity of this State, and may acquire personal property . . . by descent or purchase, and may dispose of the same, in the same manner, and to the same extent that white persons may: Provided that the provisions of this section shall not be so construed as to allow any freedman, free negro or mulatto to rent or lease any lands or tenements, except in incorporated towns or cities in which places the corporate authorities shall control the same. . . .

Sec. 5. . . . [E]very freedman, free negro and mulatto, shall . . . have a lawful home or employment, and shall have written evidence thereof. . . .

Sec. 7. . . . [E]very civil officer shall, and every person may arrest and carry back to his or her legal employer any freedman, free negro or mulatto, who shall have quit the service of his or her employer before the expiration of his or her term of service without good cause. . . .

Mississippi Vagrancy Law

Sec. 2. . . . [A]ll freedmen, free negroes and mulattoes in this State, over the age of eighteen years, found on the second Monday in January, 1866, or thereafter, with no lawful employment or business, or found unlawfully assembling themselves together either in the day or night time, and all white persons so assembling with freedmen, free negroes or mulattoes, or usually associating with freedmen, free negroes or mulattoes on terms of equality, or living in adultery or fornication with a freedwoman, free negro, or mulatto, shall be deemed vagrants, and on conviction thereof, shall be fined in the sum of not exceeding, in the case of a freedman, free negro, or mulatto, fifty dollars, and a white man two hundred dollars, and imprisoned at the discretion of the court, the free negro not exceeding ten days, and the white man not exceeding six months. . . .

Sec. 5. . . . [I]n case any freedman, free negro or mulatto, shall fail . . . after the imposition of any fine . . . to pay the same, . . . it shall be, and is hereby made the duty of the sheriff of the proper county to hire out said freedman, free negro or mulatto, to any person who will, for the shortest period of service, pay said fine . . . .

Debate over African American Rights: The Civil Rights Act

Republicans insisted that all Americans, regardless of color, were entitled to the basic rights of citizenship. In response to the black codes and other deprivations of rights in many states, North and South, they proposed a civil rights act.

Congress passed the Civil Rights bill on 15 March 1866, with southern congressmen still not permitted to take their seats. The bill made it a crime for anyone acting "under the color of law" or "custom" to deny the rights specified in Section 1. It also allowed those denied their rights in the states to transfer civil and criminal cases to the federal courts.

President Johnson vetoed the Civil Rights bill, giving his reasons in the message excerpted below from The Congressional Globe, 39th Congress, 1st Session, 1679-81 (27 March 1866).

To the Senate of the United States:

I regret that the bill which has passed both Houses of Congress . . . contains provisions which I cannot approve, consistently with my sense of duty to the whole people and my obligations to the Constitution of the United States. . . .

By the first section of the bill, all persons born in the United States, and not subject to any foreign Power, excluding Indians not taxed, are declared to be citizens of the United States. This provision comprends the Chinese of the Pacific States, Indians subject to taxation, the people called Gypsies, as well as the entire race designated as blacks, people of color, negroes, mulattoes, and persons of African blood. . . .

The right of Federal citizenship thus to be conferred on the several excepted races before mentioned, is now, for the first time, proposed to be given by law. If, as is claimed by many, all persons who are native-born already are, by virtue of the Constitution, citizens of the United States, the passage of the pending bill cannot be necessary to make them such. If, on the other hand, such persons are not citizens, as may be assumed from the proposed legislation to make them such, the grave question presents itself, whether when eleven of the thirty-six States are unrepresented in Congress, at this time it is sound policy to make our entire colored population and all other excepted classes citizens of the United States? Four millions of them have just emerged from slavery into freedom. Can it be reasonably supposed that they possess the requisite qualifications to entitle them to all the privileges and immunities of citizens of the United States? . . .

Thus a perfect equality of the white and black races is attempted to be fixed by Federal law in every State of the Union, over the vast field of State jurisdiction covered by these enumerated rights. . . . In the exercise of State policy over matters exclusively affecting the people of each State, it has frequently been thought expedient to discriminate between the two races. By the statutes of some of the States, northern as well as southern, it is enacted, for instance, that no white person shall intermarry with a negro or mulatto. . . .

Hitherto every subject embraced in the enumeration of rights contained in this bill has been considered as exclusively belonging to the States. They all relate to the internal policy and economy of the respective States. . . .

In all our history, in all our experience as a people living under Federal and State law, no such system as that contemplated by the details of this bill has ever before been proposed or adopted. They establish, for the security of the colored race, safeguards which go infinitely beyond any that the General Government has ever provided for the white race. In fact, the distinction of race and color is, by the bill, made to operate in favor 'of the colored and against the white race. They interfere with the municipal legislation of the States, with the relations existing exclusively between a State and its citizens, or between inhabitants of the same State_an absorption and assumption of power by the General Government which, if acquiesced in, must sap and destroy our federative system of limited powers, and break down the barriers which preserve the rights of the States. It is another step, or rather stride, towards centralization and the concentration of all legislative powers in the national Government. The tendency of the bill must be to resuscitate the spirit of rebellion, and to arrest the progress of those influences which are more closely drawing around the States the bonds of union and peace.

Senator Trumbull's Response

Republican senator from Illinois Lyman Trumbull, managing the bill in the Senate, successfully argued for passage of the Civil Rights Act of 1866 over the president's veto. Taken from The Congressional Globe, *39th Congress, 1st Session (4 April 1866), 1756-58, 1760-61.*

What is the bill? It declares that there shall be no distinction in civil rights between any other race or color and the white race. It declares that there shall be no different punishment inflicted on a colored man in consequence of his color than that which is inflicted on a white man for the same offense. Is that a discrimination in favor of the negro and against the foreigner—a bill the only effect of which is to preserve equality of rights?

. . . Why, sir, the very object . . . is to prevent discrimination, and language, it seems to me, could not more plainly express that object and effect. It may be said that it is for the benefit of the black man because he is now in some instances discriminated against by State laws; but that is the case with all remedial statutes. They are for the relief of the persons who need the relief, not for the relief of those who have the right already; and when those needing the relief obtain it, they stand upon the precise footing of those who do not need the benefit of the law.

. . . The bill neither confers nor abridges the rights of any one, but simply declares that in civil rights there shall be an equality among all classes of citizens. . . . Each State, so that it does not abridge the great fundamental rights belonging, under the Constitution, to all citizens, may grant or withhold such civil rights as it pleases; all that is required is that, in this respect, its laws shall be impartial.

. . . This bill in no manner interferes with the municipal regulations of any State which protects all alike in their rights of person and property. . . . How preposterous, then, to charge that unless some State can have and exercise the right to punish somebody, or to deny somebody a civil right on account of his color, its rights as a State will be destroyed.

The Fourteenth Amendment

To secure African-American citizenship and rights beyond constitutional doubt, Congress passed the Fourteenth Amendment later in 1866.

Section 1. All persons born or naturalized in the United States, and subject to the jurisdiction thereof, are citizens of the United States and of the State wherein they reside. No State shall make or enforce any law which shall abridge the privileges or immunities of citizens of the United States; nor shall any State deprive any person of life, liberty, or property, without due process of law; nor deny to any person within its jurisdiction the equal protection of the laws. . . .

Section 5. The Congress shall have power to enforce, by appropriate legislation, the provisions of this article.

Frederick Douglass Argues in Favor of Black Suffrage

Even before the Civil War ended, African-American leaders and radical Republicans were insisting that the national government secure the freedmen the right to vote. By 1867 most Republicans agreed, and by 1869 they were considering a constitutional amendment to bar racial tests for voting. Frederick Douglass, the great African-American orator and newspaper editor, explained "What the Black Man Wants" to a Boston audience in 1865. Note Douglass's allusion to the fact that women did not have the right to vote at this time. Note also his brief appeal to the anti-Irish prejudices of his Republican audience.

Excerpted from The Frederick Douglass Papers—Series One: Speeches, Debates, and Interviews, Volume 4: 1864-80, *ed. John W. Blassingame and John R. McKivigan (New Haven, 1991), 62-63, 66-68.*

I have had but one idea for the last three years to present to the American people. . . . I am for the "immediate, unconditional and universal" enfranchisement of the black man, in every State of the Union. (Loud applause.) Without this, his liberty is a mockery; without this, you might as well almost retain the old name of slavery for his condition; for, in fact, if he is not the slave of the individual master, he is the slave of society, and holds his liberty as a privilege, not as a right. . . .

It may be asked, "Why do you want it? Some men have got along very well without it. Women have not this right." Shall we justify one wrong by another? That is a sufficient answer. Shall we at this moment justify the deprivation of the negro of the right to

A photograph of Frederick Douglass, ex-slave and prominent African-American political activist. (Courtesy the Library of Congress)

vote because some one else is deprived of that privilege? I hold that women as well as men have the right to vote (applause), and my heart and my voice go with the movement to extend suffrage to woman. But that question rests upon another basis than that on which our right rests. We may be asked, I say, why we want it. I will tell you why we want it. We want it because it is our right, first of all. (Applause.) No class of men can, without insulting their own nature, be content with any deprivation of their rights. We want it, again, as a means for educating our race. Men are so constituted that they derive their conviction of their own possibilities largely from the estimate formed of them by others. If nothing is expected of a people, that people will find it difficult to contradict that expectation. By depriving us of suffrage, you affirm our incapacity to form an intelligent judgment respecting public men and public measures; you declare before the world that we are unfit to exercise the elective franchise, and by this means lead us to undervalue ourselves, to put a low estimate upon ourselves, and to feel that we have no possibilities like other men. . . . [H]ere, where universal suffrage is the rule, where that is the fundamental idea of the government, to rule us out is to make us an exception, to brand us with the stigma of inferiority, and to invite to our heads the missiles of those about us. Therefore I want the franchise for the black man.

. . . It is said that we are ignorant; I admit it. But if we know enough to be hung, we know enough to vote. If the negro knows enough to pay taxes to support the Government, he knows enough to vote—taxation and representation should go together. If he knows enough to shoulder a musket and fight for the flag, fight for the Government, he knows enough to vote. If he knows as much when he is sober as an Irishman knows when drunk, he knows enough to vote, on good American principles. (Laughter and applause.)

. . . What have you asked the black men of the South, the black men of the whole country to do? Why, you have asked them to incur the deadly enmity of their masters, in order to befriend you and to befriend this government. You have asked us to call down, not only upon ourselves, but upon our children's children, the deadly hate of the entire Southern people. You have called upon us to turn our backs upon our masters, to abandon their cause and espouse yours; to turn against the South and in favor of the North; to shoot down the Confederacy and uphold the flag—the American flag. . . . And now, what do you propose to do when you come to make peace? To reward your enemies, and trample in the dust your friends? . . . Do you mean to give your enemies the right to vote, and take it away from your friends? . . . In time of trouble we are citizens. Shall we be citizens in war, and aliens in peace? Would that be just?

. . . What I ask for the negro is not benevolence, not pity, not sympathy, but simply justice.

The Nation Supports Black Suffrage

The weekly journal The Nation *was founded in 1865 to support radical solutions to the problem of restoring the Union. The journal endorsed black suffrage.*

Excerpted from "Universal Suffrage And Universal Amnesty," The Nation (29 November 1866), 430.

[T]he Federal Government is bound by every consideration of justice, honor, and decency either to see that the freedmen enjoy complete security or to furnish them with the means of protecting themselves. In other words, we are bound either to give the freedmen a police—to see that every man of whom we claim allegiance can eat or sleep in peace—or we are bound to see that he enjoys a fair share in the making of the laws and the selection of the officers who are to execute them. . . . The former of these courses is not strictly in accordance with the spirit of our institutions; the latter is. . . .

[T]he ballot will do for the negro what it does for the poor ignorant Irishman, or German, or Englishman, but no more. It will secure him against flagrant class legislation, or cruel or unusual punishments, and against all oppression which is on its face oppressive. It will do more than this; it will cause politicians and public men—sheriffs, policemen, and the whole race of functionaries, actual and expectant—to treat him with civility, even with deference. It will put a stop to outrages and assaults of various kinds on negroes, and to all open expressions of contempt for them or dislike of them. . . .

But more than this the ballot will not do for the negro. It will not make him a good judge of the value or importance of measures not bearing directly and patently on his personal comfort or convenience; it will not enable him to tell the difference between statesmen and demagogues; between honest public men and knavish public men; between his own real friends and his real enemies; to distinguish laws contrived by scoundrels for his spoliation, under a show of immediate benefit, and schemes contrived by statesmen for his permanent advantage.

Opposition to Black Suffrage

The Reconstruction Act of 1867 enfranchised both black and white southerners, with the exception of those whites who as officeholders had sworn to uphold the Constitution of the United States and then joined the rebellion. It put the southern states back under military control temporarily. In exchange for restoration to normal relations in the Union, the Reconstruction Act required each southern state to frame a new constitution that would secure equal civil and political rights regardless of race. In the following document, a number of white Alabamans protested against the process.

Excerpted from the Petition and Memorial File, Records of the House of Representatives, 40th Cong., Record Group 233, National Archives, Washington, D.C.

The White people of Alabama send this their humble petition.

We beseech your Honorable Bodies to withdraw yourselves from the influence of the passions and contests of the hour, and contemplate for a brief period, our miserable condition . . . .

. . . [I]t is well known by all who have knowledge on the subject,—that while the negroes of the South may be more intelligent and of better morals than those of the same race in any other part of the world . . . —yet they are in the main, ignorant generally, wholly unacquainted with the principles of free Governments, improvident, disinclined to work, credulous yet suspicious, dishonest, untruthful, incapable of self-restraint, and easily impelled by want or incited by false and specious counsels, into folly and crime. . . .

Are these the people in whom should be vested the high governmental functions of establishing institutions and enacting and enforcing laws, to prevent crime, protect property, preserve peace and order in society, and promote industry, enterprise and civilization in Alabama, and the power and honor of the United States? Without property, without industry, without any regard for reputation, without controul over their own caprices and strong passions, and without fear of punishment under laws, by courts and through juries which are . . . created by and composed of . . . themselves, or of those whom they elect,—how can it be otherwise than that they will bring, to the great injury of themselves as well as of us and our children,—blight, crime, ruin and barbarism on this fair land? . . .

Will you, nearly three years after the war has ended, . . . suffer a whole State full of your kindred civilized white inhabitants, not only those who had opposed the Government, but women, children, and loyal men who had adhered to it,—to be thus consigned over to the horrid rule of barbarian negroes! . . .

. . . [D]o not, we implore you, abdicate your own rule over us, by transferring us to the blighting, brutalizing and unnatural dominion of an alien and inferior race: A race which has never shown sufficient administrative capacity for the good government of even the tribes, into which it has always been broken up in its native seats; and which in all ages, has itself furnished slaves for all the other races of the earth.

The Fifteenth Amendment

To make black enfranchisement permanent and to extend it to the north, Congress passed the Fifteenth Amendment in 1869 and sent it to the states for ratification. The required number of states ratified it in 1870.

Section 1. The right of citizens of the United States to vote shall not be denied or abridged by the United States or by any

The Fifteenth Amendment gave African Americans the right to vote for the first time; however, the end of Reconstruction, followed by the rise of Jim Crow laws in the South, largely marked the end of black suffrage until the Civil Rights movement almost a century later. (Courtesy of HarpWeek.)

State on account of race, color, or previous condition of servitude.

Section 2. The Congress shall have power to enforce this article by appropriate legislation.

Violent Resistance to Equal Rights in the South

The following documents describe Klan activities from several perspectives. Amzi Rainey, a black South Carolina sharecropper, described how the Klan terrorized his family in testimony excerpted from Proceedings in the Ku Klux Trials, at Columbia, S. C. in the United States Circuit Court, November Term, 1871 *(Columbia, S.C., 1872) 279-80.*

Former Senator James Chesnut of South Carolina testified before a congressional committee investigating the Klan. Simpson Bobo, a white lawyer and jack-of-all-trades, testified before the same committee. Their testimony is excerpted from Testimony Taken by the Joint Select Committee to Inquire into the Condition of Affairs in the Late Insurrectionary States, *vol. 1 and 2*, South Carolina *(Washington, D.C., 1872) 1:446, 449, 2:796-97.*

[Amzi Rainey's Testimony]

I looked out of the window, and I see some four or five disguised men coming up, and I ran up in the loft, and they came on; come to the door; and when they come to the door, they commenced beating and knocking. "God damn you, open the door! open the door! open the door!" . . . and my wife run to one of the doors and they knocked the top hinges off of the first, and she run across the house to the other, and agin that time they got the two hinges knocked off the other door, and the bolt held the door from falling, and she got it open . . . and when they come in, they struck her four or five licks before they said a word . . . .

They asked her who lived here. She said, "Rainey—Amzi Rainey." "What Amzi Rainey? What Amzi Rainey?" And she said, "Amzi Rainey," and he struck her another lick, and says: "Where is he? God damn him, where is he?" And she says: "I don't know."

The chief organization violently opposed to equal rights for African Americans was the Ku Klux Klan, which began in 1866 and relied on intimidation, terror, and murder to enforce white supremacy. (Courtesy the Library of Congress.)

And one said: "O, I smell him, God damn him; he has gone up in the loft." He says: "We'll kill him, too," and they come up then. . . .

I was in a box, and they said: "Oh, he is in this box, God damn him, I smell him; we'll kill him!" and the other says: "Don't kill him yet;" and they took me down. This man that struck my wife first, ran back to her and says: "God damn her, I will kill her now; I will kill her out;" and the one that went after me, he says: "Don't kill her;" and he commenced beating her then; struck her some four or five more licks, and then run back and struck me; he run back to her then, and drawed his pistol, and says: "Now, I am going to blow your damn brains out;" and the one by me threw the pistol up, and says: "Don't kill her." He aimed to strike me over the head, and struck me over the back and sunk me right down. Then, after he had done that, my little daughter—she was back in the room with the other little children—he says: "I am going to kill him;" and she runs out of the room, and says: "Don't kill my pappy; please don't kill my pappy!" He shoved her back, and says; "You go back in the room, you God damned little bitch; I will blow your brains out!" and fired and shot her . . . .

. . . [A]nd then they took me . . . [o]ff up the road, about a hundred and fifty yards; and they wanted to kill me up there, and one said, "No, don't kill him, let's talk a little to him first." Then, he asked me which way did I vote. I told him I voted the Radical [Republican] ticket. "Well," he says, "now you raise your hand and swear that you will never vote another Radical ticket, and I will not let them kill you." And he made me stand and raise my hand before him and my God, that I never would vote another Radical ticket . . . .

[Ex-Senator Chesnut's Testimony]

There is a deep dissatisfaction . . . in the hearts of the people of this State. . . . Three hundred thousand white people here around us, who had been accustomed to self-government, who had had an orderly government and had participated in that government, whose property had been taxed only by those who paid the taxes, beheld the whole thing suddenly subverted and themselves placed at the mercy of ignorance and of corruption . . . . These people are under an absolute despotism, and you will find that the countries where governments are most despotic are precisely those in which secret associations appear; small associations of parties ardent and seeking redress for real or fancied wrongs which they think cannot be avenged through the government. That is the true secret of this thing.

[Simpson Bobo's Testimony]

We have gone through one of the most remarkable changes in our relations to each other that has been known, perhaps, in the history of the world. The negro that was our slave has become our master suddenly . . . ; the bottom rail has got on top . . .—any one living here and knowing all about it, will be surprised that there has been as little disturbance as there has been. If the Government had give us a good government; if it had let us remain under a military government, none of these troubles would have been in this country. . . . There have been a great many . . . cases of the whipping of negroes in this county and some of the adjoining counties, some for one purpose and some for another. I think some of them have been political, and some of them have been with a view of answering special ends. . . . [T]he lower class of white people have a great prejudice against the negro, because he is a competitor for common labor, and wherever they come into collision, these fellows form themselves into a Klan, and take up negroes that come in their way, and punish them. . . . [F]or instance, a white man rents a tract of land to a negro. Some white man wants to get the land. The owner prefers giving it to the negro. For the purpose of punishing the negro, he will then get up a parcel of neighbors, and in disguise they will go and whip the negro half to death.

The Supreme Court Limits the Ability of the Federal Government to Protect Rights

In a series of cases interpreting the Fourteenth Amendment, the justices of the Supreme Court made it difficult for the federal government to protect the rights of American citizens in the south. In the Slaughter-House Cases, the Court distinguished between the rights people held as citizens of the United States and those they held as citizens of their states. The rights Americans thought of as basic to citizenship were those they held as state citizens, not as citizens of the United States. The Fourteenth Amendment, the justices said, only authorized the federal government to protect the latter.

Abridged from the Slaughter-House Cases, *83 U.S. 36, at 72-78 (1873).*

The Slaughter-House Cases

The first section of the fourteenth article . . . opens with a definition of citizenship—not only citizenship of the United States, but citizenship of the States. . . . It declares that persons may be citizens of the United States without regard to their citizenship of a particular State, and it overturns the Dred Scott decision by making all persons born within the United States and subject to its jurisdiction citizens of the United States. . . .

It is quite clear, then, that there is a citizenship of the United States, and a citizenship of a State, which are distinct from each other, and which depend upon different characteristics or circumstances in the individual.

We think this distinction and its explicit recognition in this amendment of great weight in this argument, because the next paragraph of this same section . . . speaks only of privileges and immunities of citizens of the United States, and does not speak of those of citizens of the several States. . . .

The language is, "No State shall make or enforce any law which shall abridge the privileges or immunities of citizens of the United States." It is a little remarkable, if this clause was intended as a protection to the citizen of a State against the legislative power of his own State, that the word citizen of the State should be left out when it is so carefully used, and used in contradistinction to citizens of the United States, in the very sentence which precedes it. It is too clear for argument that the change in phraseology was adopted understandingly and with a purpose.

Of the privileges and immunities of the citizen of the United States, and of the privileges and immunities of the citizen of the State, . . . it is only the former which are placed by this clause under the protection of the Federal Constitution . . . .

The latter must rest for their security and protection where they have heretofore rested . . . .

[The Court then quoted an earlier lower court decision that defined the privileges and immunities of state citizenship:]

"What are the privileges and immunities of citizens of the several states? We feel no hesitation in confining these expressions to those privileges and immunities which are fundamental; which belong of right to the citizens of all free governments, and which have at all times been enjoyed by citizens of the several states which compose this Union. . . . They may all . . . be comprehended under the following general heads: protection by the government, with the right to acquire and possess property of every kind, and to pursue and obtain happiness and safety, subject, nevertheless, to such restraints as the government may prescribe for the general good of the whole."

. . . Was it the purpose of the 14th Amendment, by the simple declaration that no state should make or enforce any law which shall abridge the privileges and immunities of citizens of the United States, to transfer the security and protection of all the civil rights which we have mentioned, from the states to the Federal government? And where it is declared that Congress shall have the power to enforce that article, was it intended to bring within the power of Congress the entire domain of civil rights heretofore belonging exclusively to the states?

... We are convinced that no such results were intended by the Congress which proposed these amendments, nor by the legislatures of the states, which ratified them.

Civil Rights Cases

In the Civil Rights Cases, the Court ruled that the Fourteenth Amendment only authorized the federal government to protect people against deprivations of their rights by state officials or people acting under color of state authority.

Abridged from Civil Rights Cases, 109 U.S. 3, at 10-11 (1883).

The first section of the Fourteenth Amendment ... is prohibitory in its character, and prohibitory upon the States. It declares that:

"No State shall make or enforce any law which shall abridge the privileges or immunities of citizens of the United States; nor shall any State deprive any person of life, liberty, or property without due process of law; nor deny to any person within its jurisdiction the equal protection of the laws."

It is State action of a particular character that is prohibited. Individual invasion of individual rights is not the subject-matter of the amendment. ... [T]he last section of the amendment invests Congress with power to enforce it by appropriate legislation. To enforce what? To enforce the prohibition. ... This is the legislative power conferred upon Congress, and this is the whole of it. It does not invest Congress with power to legislate upon subjects which are within the domain of State legislation; but to provide modes of relief against State legislation, or State action, of the kind referred to. It does not authorize Congress to create a code of municipal law for the regulation of private rights. ...

The Effect of "Redemption" on Black Southerners

The Supreme Court's narrow interpretation of the Fourteenth Amendment made it difficult to prosecute southern violence. Between 1873 and 1875, the resolve of the federal government to protect the rights of citizens in the south waned. By 1877, southern white Democrats regained control of southern state governments. Southern whites referred to their success as "redemption," and they used fraud in many states to prevent Republicans from regaining power. The following plea from

The return of control of state government to southern white Democrats resulted in conditions that, according to this Thomas Nast cartoon, were worse than slavery for American blacks. (Courtesy of the Library of Congress.)

Wilson H. Williams for help from the national government suggests how the change affected African Americans in the South. It had been illegal to teach slaves to read or write, so Williams's literacy, with all its spelling errors, was quite an accomplishment.

From Wilson H. Williams to Senator John Sherman, care of Rev. John D. Haynes, 15 January 1879, John Sherman papers, Manuscript Division, Library of Congress, Washington, D.C.

We poor coul[ored] men have got no more show then a good Dog. The White people is tareing all over the land picking up the poor coul men acreing [forcing] them back to thar old Homes giving them no triel but butchering them up for things that [got] don in 20 and 30 years a go. God hoe [who] made the wourld knows that it is not rite and we know you all ought to do sum thing for ous for we are healpletts cant do eney thing nor say eney thing [P]lease you all stop that thing for it has been going on long anuffe. . . .

Questions

---

1. *Describe the issues of social justice that affected the lives of free African Americans at the time the Civil War broke out.*
2. *Why did President Andrew Johnson oppose the Civil Rights Act? Did it discriminate in favor of African Americans, as he charged?*
3. *What reasons did proponents of African-American suffrage give for supporting it? Aside from the racism of the petition, did the petitioners have a point about enfranchising former slaves so soon after emancipation? How would Frederick Douglass have answered? Given the hostility of white southerners toward equal civil rights for African Americans, what would you have done to secure their rights?*
4. *To what degree were the Supreme Court decisions interpreting the Fourteenth Amendment consistent with the spirit in which they were passed?*
5. *Over all, to what degree did the civil status of African Americans change during the era of Reconstruction? How much did their status improve? What were the limitations of the change?*

FURTHER READING

The standard, prize-winning work on Reconstruction in general, providing a wealth of information about the effort to restore the Union on the basis of equality of rights, is Eric Foner's *Reconstruction: America's Unfinished Revolution, 1863-1877* (New York, 1988). A briefer and more focused work is Foner's "Rights and the Constitution in Black Life during the Civil War and Reconstruction," *Journal of American History* 74 (December 1987): 863-83. Herman Belz addresses constitutional questions more directly than Foner in *Emancipation and Equal Rights: Politics and Constitutionalism in the Civil War Era* (New York, 1978). Peyton McCrary offers another argument for the radicalism of Republican Reconstruction policy in "Republican Ideas about Politics and Social Change," *Civil War History* 30 (December 1984): 330-50. Robert J. Kaczorowski criticizes the Supreme Court for retreating from the Republican commitment to rights in *The Politics of Judicial Interpretation: The Federal Courts, Department of Justice, and Civil Rights, 1866-1876* (New York, 1985).